The Ten Demandments

For Husband, Wife, Children, and Self

LORETTA J. WOMACK

CONTENTS

WHO AM I?

By the Wife, Mother, Grandmother, Great-Grandmother and Founder of the Determined Grandmothers in Las Vegas, Nevada

I Am My Family's Keeper!

Aka: Loretta J. Womack

I am born to love, forgive, lead, guide, honor, respect, protect, and direct my family at all times.

I am the chosen one by God, therefore I vow to do as God has called me on a mission to do for them.

I will always do my part and give them back to God when my time is up!

Thank You, our heavenly Father, for trusting me to raise them and to always be able to advise them while here on earth, and for allowing them to give me my flowers while I live, amen.

My Old Testimony

TO THE READER

I wrote this book so that even a child could read and understand it. I did that so just in case my children never get around to reading and showing it to my grandchildren and great, great grandchildren someday they can pick it up themselves and read it. As you can see I have quite a large variety in age. From newborn to twenty-five year old grandchildren and great grandchildren. I birth my share of serving one of the main purposes here on earth as a woman and I am sure our family will birth much more.

INTRODUCTION
Curses Are Meant To Be Broken

Our biggest curse to be broken as a family was of not knowing God and not having a personal relationship with Him. We are all still working on breaking our family curses.

These curses were passed down and they are called pride and stubbornness—our deadliest sins.

The other curse we had to break was not getting a high school diploma or completing our education. Our purpose is just to get our lives together to the best of our ability for the crowns we will receive in heaven.

I dedicate this book to my entire family, past, present and future.
May all of you live a better life by making better
choices than the generations before you.

My Children
Harold
Gregory
Tyree
William
Andrew
Cassandra

Grandchildren
Romon
Sharaya
Donnell
Darian
Dylan
Emonie
Charlea
Shatara
Marcus
Makayla
Madisyn
De'Mornai
Tiera
Nehemiah
Leilani
Omarius
Kileek
Denaesjah
Emerald
Rosias
Dejon

Great Grand Children:
Sunti, Amira Tony, Tien
and the rest of all our generations to come.

FOUR GENERATIONS,
Plus One More

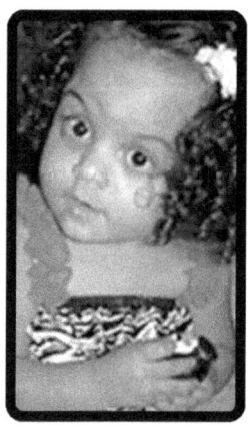

Be Faithful, Not Fearful

We are a family who broke and is still breaking all their generational curses, by supporting and teaching each other one step at a time.

This is a book about family giving each other their flowers before they die. I do not mean the beautiful flowers you see in the fields that God created for us so graciously. I mean the beautiful gifts that God so loving, caring and personally gave to each Mom for her to pass down to the generations of God's children.

I call these flowers from my children: my grandchildren, great grandchildren and maybe even great, great, grandchildren, if I live long enough. I also call the flowers that my children have given: Diplomas and Degrees. Last, I call flowers my children's accomplishments throughout their lives while they are down here on earth.

Now I would not ask them to give me my flowers while I live without first being an example of how to do this myself. I was determined to write this book for my family to assure them that they would know as much about me as possible to pass down to the generations to come. I put it in a book just in case someone loses it down the line, that way it will be on the bookshelves in the libraries. I also wrote this book because when my father passed away, I for some reason knew so little about him; I had a very hard time putting his obituary together, and my mother did not remember anything about her family.

My father lived to be in his nineties and I only knew one hand full about his relatives. Both of my grandparents were deceased before I was born. Well I did not want my family and my generations to go through that. So this book is for my family and anyone else who can learn from it.

MY ACCOMPLISHMENTS

I was, and still am a very determined person. When I make up my mind to do something, I get it done. Below is a list of some of determinations in spite of my hard time and mistakes. In this book, whenever you see me use the word *I* or *G'N'I*, I mean (per Phil 4:13), which stands for *God* and *I*. See my logo.

1. Graduate and got my diploma in spite of having my first child before I graduated. I promised my father I would get my diploma because he and my mother didn't.

2. I was determined to have a girl after having five boys.

3. I was determined to raise all six of my children and make sure they got their education by at least getting a diploma. This was accomplished by all except one who I am still proud of because even though I haven't gotten a diploma from him, he turned out to be a very hard working young man all his life so far.

4. I was determined to fully retire after a 30 year career at the telephone company to raise enough money to raise my

children and have enough for my pension, health and life insurance so my children wouldn't have to take care of me.

5. I was determined to become a professional model after having six children and several grandchildren.

6. I was determined to get a marriage right after three tries. And now I am very happily married to a wonderful man I believe God sent to me. His name is Kenneth L. Womack.

7. I was determined to use my talents and give back to the community by mentoring children. I learned how to produce fashion shows to have fashion show fund raisers for churches, schools, recreation centers and raise thousands of dollars for the scholarships. I even met Mr. Lou Rawls at one of the UNCF fundraisers (See photo below).

8. I was determined to find a blood match for a poster child, who had sickle cell by doing a blood drive when I worked at the telephone company.

9. I sponsored a Miss Black USA contestant from Colorado in 2003

10. I also sponsored Mr. Armindo Paulino Tivane, from the Mozambique Field Office, through save the children.

There are 100's of accomplishments that God has blessed me to fulfill and that I am still doing. I have worked in the community for many, many years and have given back for over twenty-six of those years.

My top 10 accomplishments were listed because I felt they were important to show and tell all my children and generations to come.

We were not brought into this world to be idle. We were not created from God just for ourselves. We were meant to develop the talents that God gave each one of us personally to help this world be a better place and to pass it down to the next generations.

It is our obligation to do the best that we can while we are here on earth, in spite of our mistakes. Just never, give up and keep trying to get life right, during and after the good and bad times in your life. If God waited for all of us to be perfect, we would never fulfill God's purpose for our birth. So get busy. If I can accomplish all these things, so can you and more. We must Get It Done!

G'N'I (God and I) even invented a Sports and Soaps TV Remote Finder. This led me to create a corporation after my father's last name. It was a way to remind us all of the Binkley family name.

So you see there is always work to be done and I never give up. (See brochure below).

My present projects are:

Getting this book published for the family. I want to complete another book called *Keeping It Real Natural*, I also want to create a magazine for Teen's called *LW's Teens Choice* as an educational guidance tool for teen's to communicate and stay anonymous to feel comfortable about asking questions and getting answers. These would be the questions that they have always wanted to ask but were too shy or afraid to do so. Certified professionals would answer these questions.

Please read this letter from one of my children, confirming I was on the right track trying to raise my children to the best of my ability. This is a letter for you Mom, on Christmas.

First, I want to thank you for all that you have gone through in your life. It has not only made you stronger; the great impact has had a great effect on all of us, which is transferable to the whole world. I love you for it and love God for allowing it to happen. The purpose of this letter (which I will write everyone a letter for Christmas) is to let you know how I feel.

Mom, you are the most amazing person I know. You have been through the ground, around the mountain, under the water, and over the Hill. You are a very blessed person, and what makes that so better is that you realize it, and share your gift with everyone. Most people only share their gift with close loved ones, but you are different. You know how to be unbiased and to let your light shine through the dark, no matter what. That takes more than you realize.

You realize it but I don't think you know to what extent. The purpose of a mother is to teach her children to love like Jesus; and that you have instilled in all your children, grandchildren, your parents, and your peers. You are truly an inspiration to all. I never thought that statement would have such a strong impact on me as it does when I think of you being the one that is an inspiration. People from all over, of different types have mentioned this to me. I never really took notice until now. I mean I have always noticed it but now as I am growing up and things are getting a little tougher, I realize how strong you were to uphold your morals and to still be an inspiration to people who did not even deserve it. I am one of those people.

I realize now every feeling you had for me during conversations, arguments, and times when I was not even around you. I know as your only daughter, I probably stayed on your mind. I realize now that everything you have done was because of love. It takes a lot of love-to-love someone unconditionally but you did it. You did what God has asked of you and even passed it on, as you should have.

That takes a lot as well. You really are a good servant and not only does God appreciate it, everyone around you does as well. How does it feel to walk the way he wants' you to after everything you have been through? How does it feel to know that when you go to Heaven, you will have God personally say "GOOD JOB SERVANT"? It will feel great, will it not?

Everything you stand for is positive and anything other than that cannot even touch you. I want to be just like that, and I know I will be. I never wanted you to die, but you did. To me you are now immortal. You are a saved person and you accomplished your biggest mission. You will never stop serving the Lord. You cannot; you are one of His. I will see you up there! I will see everyone. We are all going to be together and you can take credit for being that backbone. Of course, GOD provided all the ways; you just listened and followed. I THANK AND LOVE GOD... I THANK AND LOVE YOU. I will never forget your love.

I cannot apologize for all the things that I did to you because it will not matter. What I can say is, I understand them now and for the rest of my life I will work every day to change my bad ways and think of the one who inspired me. (It will not be easy but I will do it.) I also know you did not always have an answer but you always had a good idea. You are always supportive. For that all your kids will receive joy. Your kids will pass joy. At the end, you are the parade leader of a great foundation. That is better than leading a million-man march. You lead a mass parade for the LORD, and your family is right behind you. No reward is better than the reward you hold.

I Love you, mom, and I do not want you to forget it. It is hard to express my love all the time, but all the time I love you. I promise I will always remember what you have taught me, and I promise I will carry your legend. Remember when I said I wanted to be a legend.... well it's because I was taught by a legendary person and nothing would hurt me more than to let that die. It will never die! It is also immortal.

From Parent to Child

I can give you life, but I cannot live it for you.

I can teach you things, but I cannot make you learn.

I can give you directions, but I cannot be there to lead you.

I can allow you freedom, but I cannot account for it.

I can take you to church, but I cannot make you believe.

*I can teach you right from wrong, but I
cannot always decide for you.*

*I can offer you advice, but I cannot accept it for you. I
can give you love, but I cannot accept it for you.*

I can teach you to share, but I cannot make you unselfish.

I can teach you respect, but I cannot force you to show honor.

*I can advise you about your friends, but
I cannot choose them for you.*

I can advise you about sex, but I cannot keep you pure.

I can tell you the facts of life, but I can't build your reputation.

I can tell you about drink, but I can't say NO for you.

I can warn you about drugs, but I can't prevent your using them.

I can tell you about lofty goals, but I can't achieve them for you.

I can tell you about kindness, but I can't force you to be gracious.

I can warn you about sins, but I cannot make your morals.

I can love you as a child, but I cannot place you in God's family.

I can pray for you, but I cannot make you walk with God.

I can teach you about Jesus, but I cannot make Jesus your Lord.

*I can tell you how to live, but I cannot give
you Eternal Life… "It's Your Choice"*

Author Unknown

Loretta Juanita Womack was born June 27, 1951 to Herman Theodore Binkley and Helen King in Denver, Colorado.

My father and stepmother, Viola Binkley, raised me. I grew up in Denver and graduated from Manual High School. I started working as a babysitter and housekeeper around our neighborhood at the age of sixteen. At the age of seventeen, I worked at Lowry Air Force Base as a librarian and at the East-side Neighborhood Health Center filling pillboxes and cough syrup bottles in the pharmacy department.

When I turned eighteen, I worked during my lunch hour in the school office on the switchboard as an operator. Immediately after I graduated, I started my 30-year career at Mountain Bell Telephone Co. I retired after 30 years and opened my own business as a clothes retailer. I started modeling after my last child, Cassandra, turned two years old. I am now 61 years old and very, very blessed. I live in Las Vegas, Nevada and I am married to my wonderful husband, Kenneth L. Womack who is also a wonderful grandpa and a great addition to our family.

God thank you for my family, you blessed and trusted me with to oversee and love. I love each one of them so much and I am very proud to be the beginning of this generation. They are the greatest gift you have given to me on this earth. I have given them back to you now because they are grown up and I look forward to our reunion in heaven when it is time where we will all be together once again and for all eternity because Jesus is our Savior.

THANK YOU GOD
for Sending Me A Good Man

Loretta J. and Kenneth L. Womack

THANK YOU GOD
for Our Flock!

Our Loving Family

MY PRAYER
to All My Children

Our Father, God, and my Lord and Savior, Jesus Christ, whom I love so very, very much. Thank you for such a beautiful, big family. Words cannot express how grateful I am. I thank you, God, each day and night for all of my gifts that you allowed me to give birth to.

Thank you, God, for allowing me to live long enough to see five generations. What a blessing. These gifts of children that you have given me mean the world to me. I want to show and tell them as much as I can to testify how awesome you are, God. Thank you, God, for your unconditional love. Thank you, God, for your mercy and grace. Thank you so very, very much for sending your only begotten son and my Lord and Savior, Jesus Christ, down to us to sacrifice his life for us so that we may be born again and saved by the Father, Son, and Holy Ghost. Please, children, follow his way and let his will be done, in the name of my Lord and Savior, Jesus Christ. Amen.

My Message To My Children

Keep it simple, because complicate intimidates.

SMALL BEGINNINGS

My Children

Harold
Gregory
Tyree
William
Andrew
Cassandra

PERSONAL LETTERS

First, let me say this right now. Always remember that throughout this entire book I will be saying **I**. Every time I use the word **I**, read it as the words God and I. Remember my created logo called **G'N'I** that means **God** and **I**. Since, I could not have done anything without Him. None of us can.

Read what happened throughout the book when I used I without the *G'N'I*. Then remember only what you do for God, will last. Remember Mark 10:27: "And Jesus looking upon them said, with men it is impossible, but not with God, for with God all things are possible." KJV

Remember, even with my mistakes, G'N'I kept trying 'til we got it right. As of now, I want you to remember the word, "all" as it is in the Bible, and how many times it is used and to take it literally. When God said all, he meant all. Believe it.

I never demanded any of you to have a very high IQ. I just insisted on you having enough of a basic IQ to take it to the books. Remember that knowledge is in the books, starting with the number one best seller, the **Bible**. The Bible is your book of rights.

You have to learn that. It has all you need. All other books are books of words. The book, The Bible should be the book of your desire. Always pray before reading it that God will give you the wisdom to understand it and that His Will, not yours, will be done.

Warning: Sometimes people with too high of IQ's take the credit away from God. It all belongs to God, not to you or me.

Love You All.

Mom

Dearest Son **Harold,**

You were my firstborn. I loved you so much the moment I felt your little warm body placed up on my chest by the doctor before they cleaned you up. That was my first experience of my own little miracle.

Then you grew up and I must admit you never stopped being amazing. When you did wrong, you took your punishment and did not cry like a baby. You never stopped trying to be the best you knew how to be. I may have disagreed with you, just as you may have disagreed with me, but you never stopped trying to help us all be the best you knew we could be.

You have the faith of that mustard seed. I love the way you let nothing stop you, even when I thought you should. You show leadership because you just keep trying. I have only seen you selfish one time—that is a very good record for a young man.

Mostly Harold, I like the way you try not to make the same mistakes I made when it comes to your family. You are trying something different and I hope you get better results with your family, just as I did when I changed the way my father raised me. My family came out better too, just as each generation should.

I just ask that you keep working at getting everything right according to God's Will, not yours. Please let God's Will Be Done.

Love Mom.

HAROLD'S FAMILY

To my still lost and prodigal son, **Gregory Dale Johnson, Jr.**

Thank God, God will find you. You are still and always will be my Papoose. I remember when you were a young boy you ran home crying one day because the wind blew your school papers away. They blew out of your hands and you so much wanted your mother to see them. You were so cute, Papoose. All I could do is cuddle you up in my arms and hold you tight. I love you so much.

You grew up to be different than I could ever imagine. You are one in our family's history who has worked nonstop since you started. It has been over twenty years and for that, I am so proud of you.

I know because of the many mistakes your father and I made during your upbringing, life has been difficult for you, but I have no doubt that you too will survive just as I believe all my children will; just as my brothers and sisters and I did—and we had it pretty rough too.

The key is, never give up. Find better and smarter ways to live a life God gave to us. Life is the best gift that God can give. We must learn His will and His way for us to live like our Lord and Savior, Jesus Christ.

Please learn how to forgive so you can be forgiven. As it said in the Bible, train up a child in the way that he should go and though he might stray, he will come back. KJV.

I know I did my best.

Love you, Mom

GREGORY'S FAMILY

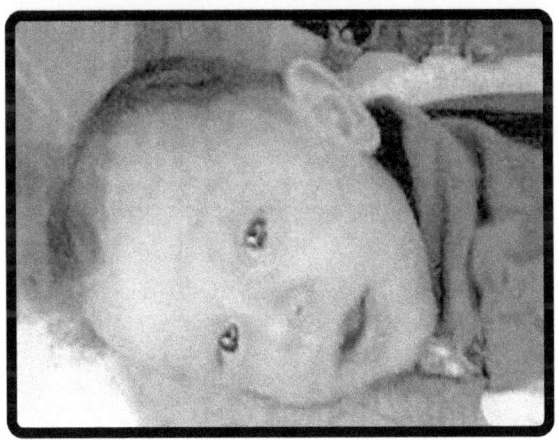

Then there was **Tyree Dathon Johnson,**

Tyree, you are more like me, except for your meanness. Thank God, you have matured. Tyree, you were the most stubborn child I had. What a man, what a man, what a mighty hard man.

I remember at church, it was you and I in the soundproof room in the back of the church. You're probably the strongest-minded child I have. That could be good and it could be bad. It proves you're not a follower of anyone but God.

You also have worked since the day you started. For that, I have always been so grateful.

But what I love so much about you is how you stick to your sacrifices until your missions are accomplished, no matter how long or how hard it might be.

Your two daughters have made you a mature young man. Your wife has challenged you in ways you never thought she would. I am sure Michelle feels that about you too. You are each other's match, and you both are still together. That says a lot about your character— dignity and respect for each other no matter what. That is quite an accomplishment that I am so impressed with, especially for so many years and I believe that for your hard work, dedication, and commitment to each other, God has truly blessed your marriage. Keep up the good work as role models.

Love Mom.

TYREE'S FAMILY

Of course, the humblest, most loving, big-hearted, over-protecting son, **William Robert Nogart Johnson,**

William, you are most sensitive. I love your gentle way of loving, caring, and taking care of anyone who will let you. You stretch your heart out to everyone. You quickly forgive. You learn fast and hard. You are an angel that spreads your wings around all of us. You shall be rewarded right here on earth and in heaven.

There has never been a time that I asked you to do something for me and you did not do it. That is almost unheard of. You hold a perfect record. THANK YOU.

You do not have an evil bone in your body. You have been a great dad to your children and stuck to them, as you should. They are a testament to your upbringing and it is showing. Their little cute faces did not stop you from exercising your responsibility to discipline them and it shows.

Your experience with relationships between a man and women could use a little work. I am sure you'll get it. Just keep studying God's way.

Your mind is quick and clever; it absorbs like a sponge. May you continue to study the word of God to learn His wisdom that he wants to pass onto you. Pass it on throughout our family for as many generations as you can. Please take better care of your body, as it is God's temple. Good health is going to hold the key to you being successful for a long time. Let God's will be done, not William's way. Amen.

Love Mom.

WILLIAM'S FAMILY

WILLIAM'S FAMILY

To my baby boy, **Andrew Theodore Johnson**

Andrew, I remember we named you after our pastor, Reverend Andrew Bowman. You were my fifth child and for sure, I wanted a girl by then instead of a boy. So, we named you after the reverend because we did not have a name picked out for a boy—only for a girl. The first moment I saw you, it was a miracle. God lit your face up like a beautiful, perfect, smooth peace color. Your cheeks were perfect. Your hair was velvet black against your beautiful complexion. Every moment of disappointment, I felt when I pushed you out because you were another boy went away. Immediately after the nurse placed you on my chest and I laid my eyes on you, it was like God said, "You wanted a girl, but let my will be done, Loretta." Thank you, God, for being God and not being Loretta.

I call you my blessed one. You were never bad. You were so good; I always waited for the day you would let it out. I knew you had bad traits in you, because there is good and bad in everyone, but it never showed up until you grew up. Then I learned you had just held it in you all those years. I thought I was just getting a break from one of my children. Actually you did give me a break because you did not let it out as a child, but as an adult you exploded. Thank God, by then I had pretty much turned you back over to Him. I prayed and I prayed not only for you, but also for all my children. Thank God, we are all God's children first and last because I know God will see you and all my children through it all just like he has and will for me. Andrew, hang in there; the bad will pass. It did for me and it will for you. Thank you, Andrew for being my most peaceful, loving, and caring son. I'll never forget the day you told all of us that we should show more love to each other by hugging and saying 'I love you' more often.

Love Mom.

ANDREW FAMILY

Cassandra, Cassandra, **Cassandra Monique Williams**

Wow! Where do I start? Okay!

You were what I always wanted and my dad told me I did not need a girl. I couldn't understand why he would tell me that. He never told me why and for some reason I never asked him why not, but as I grew, and now you're grown. I think I figured it out.

A girl is cute, precious, manipulating, sweet, loveable, sneaky, selfish, spoiled, moody, and will worry you to death—if you let her. I think that describes a girl to a T. Now I know why my father said it, especially since he had four of them himself.

I remember my dad was and will always be my hero, but the first time I saw him cry was over my big sister. I never saw my dad cry about anything. I was so used to seeing him handle almost anything that came to him, but the day my big sister left the house, my dad cried. It hurt me to see my dad cry. Girl's make you cry! They make you hurt! They disappoint you more than boys do for a reason.

I can't pretend I don't know the reason anymore. Between my daughter and myself, I know the truth is we love the girls different— then we love the boys, not more, just different. I will get back to that later because it's a whole another chapter, so back to you Miss Cassandra Williams.

First, I wanted to say you are my most challenged child. You were not just a challenge for me but the whole family—our immediate family and our church family.

I mean, look at this beautiful child. Who would have guessed that you would have been so much work to raise? You're a perfect example of the phrase, "it takes a Village to Raise a Child."

When I think back on when I was a girl growing up, if my dad knew half of the things I did, he would turn over in his grave and back again for disappointment. This too, is a chapter that I will get to later in the book.

Cassandra, you are, like Andrew was—a late bloomer. You didn't start cutting up until you were a little older. Your assigned demon— as we all have them—didn't start showing its head until about the age of five or six, then it went back into hiding until middle school. Then came high school where it matured.

I kept asking myself where I went wrong for her to act this angry, mad, destructive, selfish, and spoiled. The first thing I thought was "well, the Bible does say that what you sow you shall reap." I went to thinking back to how bad I was when I was a girl growing up and wondering if I was this bad when my parents were raising me. I said to myself, "no;" of course I didn't think I was that bad. Then I went to think further on, but they say that what you did to your parents your children you will also do to you. Not only will you sow what you reap, but 10 times more. That was the answer. My daughter did to me ten times more than I did to my dad, it was written in the Bible and I was warned. I just didn't believe it would be that bad.

The moral of this true story is be careful how you live and what you do and who you do it to.

But I must admit, Cassandra. I thank God for our bad experience together because it brought you and me closer to God. It also showed us both how a mother and daughter's relationship should be on a motherly, spiritual level; not on a friendly level like so many mothers who try to be friends with their daughters.

I thank God too that we made it through to the other side of success, through that very ugly storm alive, in the name of Jesus. Thank you, God. Amen.

Love, Mom.

CASSANDRA'S FAMILY

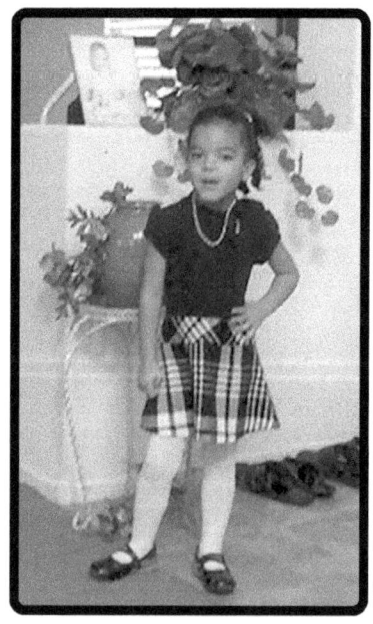

MY FLOWERS
While I Live

I am glad to get my flowers while I live from my husband and children. From my children I received five diplomas: one commercial arts degree, an Associate of Applied Science Degree in Accounting with a Minor in Computer Applications, and a son who worked ever since he left school. I can't complain.

These are my flowers and all the grandchildren are more flowers. My husband's love and moral support provided enough flowers to last me the rest of my life; my great-grandchildren are a bonus. Many people don't live to see their great-grandchildren. All of my struggles paid off. I made it. I know all my children have whatever it takes to be somebody in life. Education was my drive for them to at least graduate.

I can't say enough about my husband. I remember telling him when we met that I had six children. He thought I was lying to him and just telling him that to scare him off. I warned him if he wanted to step my way he would have to step up to a platter not just a plate. He challenged us, going now on thirteen years and still counting. I love him very much and I am proud of him. I must admit I didn't think he would last. He came into our family after all my children were grown. He got along with all of them and has even gotten along with the grandchildren and the great-grandchildren. I knew dealing with six different grown children's personalities wasn't easy. To me this is what I mean when I say "GIVE ME MY FLOWERS WHILE I LIVE." Thank you, Kenny.

I feel very Blessed and if I had to die today, I am happy and proud of my family. All of my children's achievements and having grandchildren and great-grandchildren are all the flowers that I need.

Thank you all!

Love
Loretta—Your Mom and wife

YOU CAN TRY HIM NOW
or try Him later

Note: I tried Him later, which is why I am writing this book. However, I didn't try too late and because I didn't wait too late, I am blessed and able to write and dedicate this book to my family and whoever else is reading it. This way you won't have to pay as many consequences as I did.

I really do believe that all my children are saved, (have given their life to Christ). That is why I believe I sleep so peacefully—and of course, knowing that I am saved also, and believe my husband is too, or we would not still be together.

To be saved is only the beginning of being born again, (the act of allowing God to change who you are). It is where our earthly life should start turning over to our heavenly life. It is the life that God gives us for eternity. We must realize the difference between our earthly and heavenly life. It is extremely different and we have to learn to live it differently.

Being born again is not a physical action you can see on the outside. It is a spiritual action that takes place on the inside of your heart, mind, body, and soul. You must truly accept the Holy Ghost to come inside of you and live. You must truly believe that our Lord and Savior Jesus Christ suffered like no other human could or would just for each and every one of us to have the gift of eternal life.

We were all bought and paid for by the blood of Jesus, God's only begotten Son. He is the only way to get to our loving, merciful, glorious God. You must accept Him first to be chosen by God for this wonderful gift and accept Him on your own will. No one but no one can accept Him into your life but you. There are no exceptions.

Thank you, Heavenly Father, for choosing me first. I accept you and I accepted your son as my Lord and Savior with all my life to do all of your will. Amen.

CHAPTER 1

There are no excuses.
We must get it done

My children and I are each other's worst critics. We are harder on each other about getting our lives correct far more than we are on any outsider. We don't leave any room for excuses. Even if we are not perfect, we practice sometimes too hard to be perfect. In a way it is good and in a way it is bad, but I would rather we be this way than not. This way keeps us on our toes. We love each other unconditionally. We never give up on each other. I love that about us. I learned this from my dad and stepmother and passed it on to my family. I know that even though my real mother wasn't with us, her prayers were.

I remember hearing my father say, "Nobody owes you anything. I understand if there were things that happened to you that weren't your fault when you were growing up, but when you grow up, it is your responsibility to make the correct choices. Forgive and move on. Leave the past in the past." Just do the right things God said, "Vengeance is mine".

If I would have let just half the bad things that happened to me while growing up bother me, I probably wouldn't still be living, but by the grace of my God I made it through the storms. And because my father and stepmother—may they rest in peace— weren't watching me as much as they could have, I had a tough time. If they knew half of the bad things that happened to me, they would have probably tried to kill somebody.

I don't sweat it too much because I lived to see one guy die of cancer and the other burn to death in a fire.

So this is why I tell my children to please watch their children, especially around relatives, family and friends. I am telling you to watch all my grandchildren very closely at all times, with everybody. I was one of the blessed ones. I turned myself around with the strength of God's grace. As we know, everyone is not so blessed— and remember, I mean *G'N'I*, God and *I*

Thank you Jesus!

As we all know, I wasn't the first to be abused and I won't be the last. I pray for everyone and myself all the time. Life must still go on, so I learned from my mistakes and I take responsibility for doing wrong and/ or abusing. It is written that what goes around comes around. I also paid dearly for shortcomings. Thank God, I had repented at a very early age and my streak was short.

By the grace of God, I no longer let my past dictate my future. God is good all the time.

Believe it or not, I do practice more than I preach to do the will of God. I try so hard to be the role model that God wants me to be for my family and anyone else who is watching me. I pray that my children do the same. Get rid of the excuses for how I fell short of raising you and just do the right thing by God. Be all that you can be, which is even more than I have been. Be better, and then I'll be happy and blessed.

We have to get it right. There are no excuses.

CHAPTER 2

We love the girls different, not more, just different

A note to you Cassandra: No disrespect or offense to you, but this is how I saw it. Maybe someday you will tell our story of how you saw it.

I want to start out with my daughter. I only have one girl. I love her different, not more than her brothers. Cassandra in many ways is like her mom. I love the fact that she watched me like a hawk when growing up. She stuck to me like glue. To this day she still watches me that way; so do her brothers. In knowing this I have always tried to be the best in everything I do, but we all make mistakes.

Mistake number one: I tried too hard with Cassandra because she was the only girl. I gave her too much too soon. Her dad and I ended up getting a divorce and I tried to be her mom, father, sister-that-she-never-had growing up, and a best friend. That was mistake number two.

I made a promise to her because she was such a good little girl and very smart. She was testing out at fourth grade math in her kindergarten class. She attended Union Baptist Excel Institute. She made very good grades and I told her if she kept good grades until she got old enough to drive a car that I would buy her one. So, she did and I did. I bought her a nice red, shiny car. This was mistake number three.

Last but not least. My worst mistake, number four: I loved her too much. Now, you probably think you could never love your children too much, but you can. Let me explain:

I remember seeing my father cry for the very first time over my older sister, Ruth. I didn't understand his tears for her until I grew up and had my own daughter. I even remember wanting a girl so bad because I had five boys. Actually, I was ready to have a girl after my first boy. Anyway, I remember that my father who had four of us girls said to me "you don't need a girl". Of course, I didn't understand that remark either until I had one. Girls break your heart; boys break your pocket.

I want to converse and share this information of our little experience to hopefully prevent this from ever happening again, especially in our family. Today we love each other very much, but only on a spiritual level instead of the level I thought I was supposed to love her on. I can't be a so-called father, sister, and best friend to her, but I know who can—God can. I tried to be to her what only God can be to her, which is everything and everybody. I tried to do God's work. My assignment was to birth her, raise her, and turn her back over to God. I tried to keep her all to myself. I tried to be all those things to her and I failed. I learned from God the hard way that my only job was to be a mother to her.

My daughter and I were very close. I spoiled her beyond the limit. People have told me I spoil all my children that way. Anyway, not only did I spoil her beyond the limit but I over-protected her, so much to where she just automatically expected me to do whatever, whenever. Then one day it all began. God whipped me, after I whipped her.

The trouble started when she noticed that her father and I wanted to separate. Cassandra and her father were just as close as she and I, when we separated for the first time her teacher called me with bad news. Her teacher asked if everything was all right in my home because Cassandra was starting to change for the worse. She explained to me that her grades were starting to drop and a negative attitude was developing. I confessed that her dad and I were separating. I began to really see a change in Cassandra, so I made a decision to stay with her father long enough for Cassandra to get older and could hopefully understand that the divorce was necessary. In other words, just because her dad and I didn't get along, that was not her fault.

After Cassandra grew older, I figured she would handle the final separation and divorce. I was wrong. Now I realize how some people really are truly dramatized, when the major people are missing in their lives—mother and father. Now I see and understand the full purpose for mothers and fathers.

As Cassandra got into middle school, she got worse. She called the principal the "B" word. I asked her why she did that. She told me because everybody else wanted to, but they were scared. I knew then it was going to be a struggle, but I had no idea it would get much worse.

In high school, she not only got into fights at school, but she got into fights with her family. Of course, that was a sign of crying out because she was hurting inside and didn't know any other way to handle her hurt because of her parents' break up.

As she went to high school, the fights kept going. All the fights she had, she had a reason to fight back because, they were all started by the other people and she had a right to defend herself, but she would take it too personally. Her temper and patience's grew short and out of control.

It began to cost her and me heavy consequences. This is where my whipping began from God. I lacked the knowledge from the book. You know that book of rights that I told you about in the beginning of this book—the book of guidance, that book called the Bible. I heard people say there is no book on parenting. Wrong! Yes there is. It was here all along. It is not just a book on parenting. It is a book on marriage, parenting, and living. It has it all in the Bible. I just didn't know because I didn't pick up my book of rights, guidance, and all the answers.

All the answers to all things are in the book. If I had picked up the book, prayed first, and read and studied the Bible, none of this would have happened to us. However, I got it now. I learned the hard way for all of us. The purpose of this book is for God and I to pass the knowledge on to all my children; to pass it down to their children. I must share the worst that happened to us so you will know just how real all of this kind of stuff is and that it does happen.

Now for the bad news:

My daughter and I got into a real fistfight. Now in my family— meaning the Loretta Juanita Binkley Womack Family—that is a for-sure no-no. Yes, I saw it happen in my family growing up and that is why I just refused to do it myself. I hoped it would never happen to me in raising my own family, but it did. I purposely put the fear of me in my children—at least my boys—so that would never happen. Big mistake! Yes, that was one of the mistakes I made in raising my children. I should have taught them more about the fear of God, not the fear of Loretta.

Boy, did God show me! I thought after seeing a flying plate of spaghetti almost take off the top of their oldest brother's head for disobeying me that one time would scare them enough not to try to get physical with me. Well, it worked for the boys, so surely I thought it would scare my girl. Not!

I figured that after all, I had done for her and sacrificed for her that she would be the last child of mine to try me, I was so hurt. I felt some of how Jesus felt about Judas about my own daughter; of course, nowhere near to the extent that Jesus felt about Judas, but I feel that I felt some of what Jesus felt.

My daughter was hurting inside to a degree that I surely couldn't see or understand. I know now that she didn't know she had more options. I know now she lacked the knowledge of wisdom from God. I didn't even know myself, or that never would have happened. I should have known better. I would have known better had I picked up my book of rights, wisdom and understood on how to prevent that from ever happening. Oh!, I got it now. I know the way now—what to do to keep that from happening, but it cost my daughter and me a very high price. It cost my daughter and me a permanent condition that we both have to live with for the rest of our lives. Now, that's good news and bad news. The fight permanently ended a friendly relationship with her. You can't be friends with them as their mother, like so many of us try to do with our daughters—and even fathers too. I ended up not only whipping my daughter, but kicking her out of my home.

She can never come back and live with me, not ever again. She broke the vow that I had tried so hard not to break with my parents because I saw from my parents and siblings that it wasn't the answer. I hated violence. It never is the answer to anything.

Remember, violence is never the answer. Anyway, that is the bad news. I didn't know the answer to my loving, deep-hurting daughter's problem or understand the degree. If only I had just picked up the book. Surely, I know now and I hope after sharing our story with you, this will never happen to you or your family.

What happen and how did it begin? One day when my daughter felt she just couldn't take it anymore, she acted out violently. She made one of the biggest mistakes of her life.

She raised her hand up to fight. A fight is what she wanted and a fight is what she got. We fought from the down-stairs to the up-stairs for about a good 15 to 20 minutes. We were both fighting more out of frustration than anger at first. You could tell we really weren't trying to hurt each other because we never once hit each other in the face or picked up anything to try and hurt or kill each other.

I did end up getting mad at her though, because my sister was trying to break up the fight and Cassandra hit my sister in the face. I had to end the fight. I recall just letting her take her frustration out on me since I was part of her problem. I could see my baby crying and hurting and lashing out at me, but then I got angry when I saw something else for the first time in my life. I could see my poor, little, innocent child crying out for help and then I saw that demon in my child all at the same time.

The demon got a little more aggressive so I had to get a lot more aggressive in order to take over and end the fight. I hadn't remembered seeing a demon, then it came to me and I did remember, I had actually recognized this demon in another situation. I realize that I had seen this same demon before, but just didn't really understand who he was and I couldn't believe what I was seeing. I was in denial. I saw that look before in someone else and knew that something was not right. There again, had I picked up the book and learned who the demon was, I would have known then, like I do now. That demon is the devil and he is real.

People don't want to believe that we are in a spiritual war. It was very much the devil before, when I saw him face-to-face in the other people. I saw that devil in my daughter. When I saw the devil before face-to-face, (I, meaning G'N'I) had to handle him and nip him in the bud back then, with that other person, just like G'N'I had to nip that demon in the bud in my daughter. I learned how demons get into people and can get into me too. (I, meaning G'N'I) just don't let him live in me or in those whom God gave to me, which are my children. That's if I can help it. It's well-known that things can get bigger than I can handle. That is when God has to do it all, so I let go and let God do it.

Now, for the good news:

Even though my daughter and I went through such a bad experience, there were very good result. First, we both came out alive. Second, I called the police but I didn't press charges. I could have because my daughter was over 18 years old and it was my house and she was disturbing the peace, but I didn't like the choice I had of pressing charges and my child going to jail.

I wanted to know what was wrong with my child. I wanted her tested to see if something was really wrong in her brain to make her break the vow that I called myself making sure would never be broken under my roof. The officers left me no choice. They told me if I didn't press charges there was nothing they could do but leave their card for her to call them if she wanted to turn herself in and voluntarily get the test done. Of course, she didn't want to do that so I told her she had to leave, she had to move out at once.

I wasn't about to give that demon a second chance so that could happen again. Without my daughter seeking help to see what was wrong with her and getting to the root, it most likely would happened again. Cassandra might lash out at someone and she did. It cost her friends, family, jobs, and even jail time. It even almost cost our lives, but the good news is it didn't. God sent us help and rescued us with the angels from up above. You know, angels are very real too. The angels protected us and actually saved our lives. That's a whole other story. Anyway, Cassandra kept having incidents of this sort. We finally took the problem to God, which is where I should have taken it in the first place. I got down on my knees and begged God for help and answers. I prayed, the family prayed, and we finally got the answer. It came to me to go spiritual with our problem. I called my pastor. I told him what had been going on. He prayed right away and then called Cassandra. I asked him to call me back after he talked to her and let me know if he thought she need medical help.

You see, prayer is real too; it helps. After the pastor talked to her, sure enough, he had gotten to the root of my daughter's problem. I wish one day she too would write a book to explain just exactly what all took place with her to make her act that way. I cannot tell it all because I only know what I saw that caused her to act out her emotions. I don't know what all she confessed to the pastor, so I can't write it, but I do know that every since that day I received that call from the pastor, I only saw one incident around me. I heard about others from her but they were nowhere near as bad.

She is getting better. In fact, she even took an anger management class, but two things took place to make her change. One was that she wanted to change and she asked the pastor how to do it. Two was that she disciplined herself to surrender to God. I tried to make her do it, but I couldn't. She had to want to do it for herself, just as each one of us has to also. She prayed to God for his help, which is the only place where any of our help comes from.

Thank you God, for never leaving my daughter, and thank you, God, for letting my daughter come back to you, in the name of Jesus. Amen.

My daughter allowed the demons to come inside her and stay too long. She was hurt, lonesome, depressed, angry, and helpless. She felt that after her father and my divorce was over, it was the beginning and end for her. Then on top of that, growing up with five brothers was tough, not to mention not keeping a boyfriend because she was too tough on them. Then I ended up, married again and that was another blow. I think what really made her go way overboard was her breakup from her daughter's father. She thought—just like most of us mothers think—that the baby's father would last through thick and thin. Wrong.

I believe that although God never makes mistakes on who he allows to be born into the world, we women many times pick the wrong choice of men for ourselves. I myself had to get married three times before I got it right. I believe, once again, that it was because I didn't pick up the book. In the book—you know that bible book—it tells how to be a wife according to God. I wished I knew what I know now. I am mastering how to be a wife for going on five years with my current husband. I met him in January 2000 and we married in 2005. I believe I got it right this time.

Anyway, to make a long story short, I believe Cassandra had plenty to be angry about, but she should not have let her emotions run her life the way it did. It cost her allot, but she and I were forced to benefit big time from our bad experience.

The great news is that the experience forced us to grow closer to God. It helped us to grow closer to each other, but on a more spiritual level. God doesn't get jealous on that level. You see, I was whip because, I allowed my daughter to get closer to me than God. God says, "no one comes before me." No one. My mistake was that I let Cassandra come before God. I even began to realize who else and what else I let come before God. Take it from me, no one and nothing comes before God! I got it now. There have been many times; even now, I have to back up off people and things because I know not to break that commandment. So that is how I got whipped after whipping my child for the last time. I hope you all learn from our mistakes, but I thank you, Cassandra, for that Christmas letter you wrote to me assuring me that you do know what to do and how life really should be.

I enjoy her so much more on a spiritual level. I hope everyone learns how to get to that level in every relationship they have. I refuse to live with anyone who is not on a spiritual level ever again. God showed us both a lesson through each other. Thank you, God, in Jesus' Name. Amen.

After my pastor called and told me the root of her problem, Cassandra and I were able to resolve the problem we had. I thought maybe there was such things as bi-polar, even though I didn't then and still don't believe it now that she was bi-polar. I do believe a child can go so long getting their way and then have temper tantrums if they stop getting their way. I believe that children and people do what you let them do to you. I also believe that after letting them misbehave for so long that they get frustrated and violent. They allow the demon in and end up losing control. The demon then takes over and takes residence in the human body. That's when the person loses all control and starts to hurt others and even themselves sometimes. Just like so many other kids and young adults do these days.

To sum up my daughter's problem, the root began to grow when her father left. The root grew more being raised with five brothers who were a little tough on her. I remarried and she felt she was losing me too. I noticed the attitude and started withdrawing, giving her everything and her way. She started getting defensive over everything and with everybody. She started developing low self-esteem because she couldn't keep a boyfriend, she was too mean. She then trusted the baby's daddy like all of us mothers do and thought he was going to last through thick and thin, but he didn't and when he didn't that was the straw that broke the camels back.

Come to find out my daughter wasn't crazy. She didn't even need medication. After my pastor prayed and counseled her for a couple of days, he said she'll be ok. He also said she was having adult tantrums and that she just needed to make up in her mind to stop having them. I do believe she allowed the demon to stay in her too long. I also believe that all our prayers prayed the demon out of her, including her praying for herself and surrendering herself back to God. She had left God and it showed. She just needed to repent and she needed Jesus. Thank you, God, for allowing her to come back to you. Amen.

I believe our lesson from God was, to give us a second chance to get a bad situation right by Him first and each other second. Some mothers and daughters don't get that second chance to forgive so they can be forgiven. My daughter is the only person who drew me further away from God and closer to God.

Thank you God for making me understand that you are in control at all times. I love you for the mistake that you showed us how to turn it around and make it turn out for the good.

Oh, by the way I did let my daughter come back home again to get back on her feet. Now she is doing well.

My New Testimony

THE 10 DEMANDMENTS
that a Woman Demands of Her Man

1. You must love God and have a relationship with Him that keeps Him number one.

2. You must know your purpose, who you are, whose you are, and who the enemy is.

3. You must know how to communicate by talking less and listening more.

4. You must keep yourself healthy until death do us part.

5. You must be wise enough to have at least a high school diploma.

6. You must be fearless of earthly things in order to fight all our spiritual battles and win the war.

7. You must be humble enough to admit when you're wrong and to apologize.

8. You must not force, fight, or divorce me.

9. You must be a man of love, honesty, honor, respect, and integrity in character.

10. You must submit to God before asking and expecting me to submit to you.

1. One of a man's biggest mistakes is not knowing who or whose he is. You must get to know yourself and your Creator to have a relationship with Him. Many men go through life clueless about themselves and life. Therefore they never learn what God's plan is for them and that they are here for God's purpose—not their own. They don't know that it all begins with God's love for us and the love we should have for God and others in order for our lives to work out for the best. None of us ask to be here. God has already planned our journeys here on the earth. And it is His will that we be here. You must establish a relationship with God in order to understand what He expects you to do for God and His people, not just for yourself. Not only must you love God but you must love Him with all your heart, soul, mind, and body. You must also then love your neighbor as thyself. Read all about it in Matthew 22:36–40. You must learn to love yourself, your wife, your children, and others the way God intended for you to—not the way you want to. We women want a man to commit to marrying us, not to shacking up with us. *We women demand a man!*

2. Everyone should want to know what their purposes are, both to please God and in order for us to be pleased. Some people just live to exist, never even finding out their purposes. I know of a man who lived to be fifty and never found his purpose, so he lived a miserable life.

If you don't know your purpose, how can you live out your life and expect anyone to follow you? How can you set goals for yourself, for your wife, and for your children and expect them to follow you if you don't know where you're going or even how to get there? Some men develop low self-esteem and feel sorry for themselves because of their bad upbringing from their parents; then they can go into a depression, end up having a family, and take it out on the family. That's not right, nor is it fair to their families. They end up getting cheated out of the abundant life God intended for them and their family. Your life and theirs is the greatest gift God gave, so don't cheat yourself and them out of life.

Once you are born, you have a choice and obligation to fulfill your life with abundance while here on the earth. It should be an honor considering how blessed we are to be chosen by God even to be here. We should be more than happy to complete God's missions that He has assigned to us. You are bought and paid for by the blood of Jesus, and therefore you belong to God and not yourself. You must be born again to be led by the Holy Spirit for wisdom and understanding about what it is that you are to do for God—to know your purpose. You will understand who the devil is and who your enemies are, and you will learn how to defeat them and protect yourself and your family at all times.

Get to know Jesus, who is the truth and the life, so that you will be set free and able to lead your family to freedom!

3. Many men think they know how to communicate. They talk better than they listen. They don't want to take the time to listen; nor do they realize that in order to communicate, you have to learn when to talk and when to listen and that you really do learn much more by listening more than by talking.

From my experience, men speak over women and sometimes don't even allow a woman to voice her opinion, which we all have a right to do in a relationship. I will never again be in a relationship without being able to voice my opinion. I also won't be in a relationship if my man doesn't own and voice his opinion.

That is the whole idea of being in a relationship, otherwise you should keep to yourself. How else would you learn about each other or how to please each other if you don't learn how to communicate? For many years I had bad relationships because of a lack of knowing how to communicate. It is one of the biggest reasons for a divorce. Learn how to communicate instead of interrupting while your partner is still speaking because you're so busy wanting to get your point across and afraid you're not going to get to speak that you don't even hear what the other one is saying. Instead of just waiting your turn and listening, you're too busy thinking about what you want to say. You should wait until the other person is finished so you both can be heard and get your points across; you both should be man and woman enough to hear each other out. You'll have a better conversation and a better chance of coming to an agreement, even if you have to agree to disagree. Or just be man enough to know which decision is the better one instead of worrying about whether it's her idea or yours. Remember that God gave woman five senses too—for a reason. Don't believe the myth that just because you're the man, your decision is always the right one.

4. There is no way to have a healthy marriage if you're unhealthy emotionally, mentally, physically, sexually, financially, and especially spiritually. It can cause dysfunction to happen in your relationship. You must have a good diet and nutrition so that your brain, main organs, five senses, and all body parts will function well on a daily basis.

God created every kind of good food for your body to function properly. Do your research on the right foods for you, your wife, and your family. Make sure you get seven to eight hours of sleep, as that is the time when your body rejuvenates itself. Don't forget to drink half your weight in ounces of water (e.g., if you weigh

200 pounds, drink 100 ounces a day), and make sure to exercise about thirty minutes a day. Men, please get your yearly checkups at the doctor and dentist. Please take serious care of your body, which is God's temple. Overeating, drinking, and toxic intake of alcohol, drugs, and cigarettes are not good. But I am sure you know that. A lot of men love running the streets into the wee hours of the night doing something they have no business doing anyway—instead of getting enough sleep and spending the proper time with their wives and children. One of the key reasons I married my husband is because he could be at home at night. The wife and children want their time. (Men, beware! Just do the right thing!)

5. College is not for everyone; however, a minimum of a high school diploma is required. It shows your first evidence of commitment, discipline, dedication, patience, and character. We can all relate to how long it seems to take to graduate from high school. But sticking with it and completing those twelve years is the honorable thing to do. It was one of the best choices I made in my life. And I got blessed because I got one of the better jobs that my friends who went to college wished they could have got. If you can't complete that first step of adulthood, your future could be dim, hard, and complicated. Failure is more likely if you don't at least graduate on time to get a fair start in life. Barack Obama said, "If you think education is expensive, wait till you see how much ignorance is going to cost you."

6. After getting an education, you can build character and cultivate values like courage, faith, belief, and fearlessness. If a man fears no one and nothing but God, that is half of the battle. I understand getting married is intimidating for a man or a woman and makes you feel like you have to give up your freedom, money, family,

and friends. But it is doable if you stay steadfast at it and put God first in your marriage. You actually gain a lot more than you had—just don't put anything or anybody before God.

Fear is the number-one tool that the devil uses to keep you from being successful. Fear makes you feel insecure. But fear not, and remember Philippians 4:13 (NKJV): "I can do all things through Christ who strengthens me." And remember—you're not single anymore nor a bachelor. So you will have to share your time and dime if you decide to get married and have children. You will be obligated to do right by God and your new additions. Just don't get married until the time is right and God sends you that right woman. Once you get married you will have to become one in God and your wife. Not one in the streets and worldly things. You will have to step up and face up to all the responsibilities that come with getting married and having children. Yes, of course you should be allowed some time for yourself, but not a lot.

Again, don't get married until the time is right. You and your family will truly benefit from the blessings that will trickle down to you and your family if you just remember to give them the quality time they deserve. Love in the way and order that God says to love. *Keeping God first—and submitting to Him—are the keys to your successful marriage and life.*

7. Before walking into marriage you must study the word of the Lord to show yourself approved. Learn how to apologize when necessary and ask for forgiveness if need to. Be willing to forgive, for it is another thing the devil (the enemy) uses to separate, divorce, rob, steal, and kill. The devil/enemy can only take what you give him. Control belongs to God and you. Don't give it away. Be a man of grace, humility, integrity, honesty and patience. *Please stay single until you are ready to do these things as a married man.*

8. Swallow your pride and never bring it up again. It has no place in a marriage or relationship. It too steals your true created identity imparted from the Creator to you. I mentioned before the importance of a man submitting to God. Gentlemen, please research the definition of *submit*. Men tend to want women to submit to them without first submitting themselves to God. Men, please don't ask your wife to submit to you if you're not submitting to God. As a matter of fact, don't even ask for her hand in marriage if you haven't already submitted to God. Read all about it in Ephesians 5:22–23. I want to follow my husband in the right direction, but he must be going in the right direction and know where he is going.

You must not force, fight or divorce. Marriage is forever till death do you part.

9. I must admit after being married three times the third one is definitely a challenge but well worth it because I know it's the last. I learned how to keep my husband. The hardest thing I have learned is how to get along with the opposite sex. God wanted me to conquer that, and I have; I've got it now. I thought having six of my babies was hard, but this beats that. I learned if you want a man, a husband, you have to take the time to get to know them and let them have the time to get to know you. Realize that they are who they are, which is not who you are, and vice versa. The best way to get along with people is to allow them to be who they are, which is who you're not. I believe I heard Joyce Meyer say that. It was some of the best advice I have received. It works. But in saying that, gentlemen, I would suggest that you wait for God to send you a lady who has as much in common with you as possible, and make sure you know you're not going to agree on everything. You're going to have to know what you can tolerate because no two people are the same. There is always going to be

something about the person you get that is not going to change, that thing that you wish they would change— and again, vice versa.

I am sure by now we women have to be at the top of a man's list, as being able to get along with us has to be one of their biggest challenges too. I refuse to turn to a woman, so a man it is because I sure don't want to grow old by myself. I think women may turn to each other just as men turn to each other because the same sex understands each other and it is easier. So they settle for the same sex. I could be wrong; that is just my opinion.

Even though it took me three times to get it right, I am glad I didn't settle for less and give up. God of course knew best, and I am glad I trusted Him. It is so awesome to get along with my husband, now that we both have decided to hang in there and work out our issues. We understand it will be an ongoing lifetime thing to do till death do us part. Of course it takes patience, sacrifice, commitment, dedication, and the love for God, myself, and my husband to make it happen as I feel my husband does the same. So gentlemen, just remember what it takes. I had to learn how to have a relationship with God, with myself, and then with my husband. Building the relationship is the key. But my husband and I both had to want it. The woman or man can't build a marriage without partnering with God first and then each other. God must be in the equation, or it will not work—no ifs, ands, or buts about it.

I know now not to ever settle for just a move-in situation. I know to do it right the first time, which is God's way, not mine or his. I tried shacking; it don't work for me. Even I learned to submit to God before husband. So it works both ways. *The key here is not to ever, ever, let violence of any kind bleed into your marriage or relationship. It doesn't belong, just as fornication and adultery don't. You must be a man of love, honor, respect, dignity, and integrity.*

10. How many times have you heard a woman say, "I am not happy in my marriage"? This is where I have to apologize to my husband and you men because I learned that my husband and no other man or human being can make me happy. My happiness only comes from the Lord! For the longest time, I was disappointed and angry because my husband could not fill the emptiness in my heart and soul that only God can fill. I only ask of my husband to submit to God before asking me to submit to him. I tried to control this issue in my life and almost got a divorce over it. But ladies, if you are reading this book, I've got it now. I want to pass it on to you, that it won't work that way. Only God!

THE 10
DEMANDMENTS
that a man demands of his wife

1. Know how to love God, yourself, your husband, and then you both as one in God.

2. Know that you have to establish a relationship with God, yourself, and your husband.

3. Know when to stop to prevent an argument and not to disrespect your husband.

4. Know you never should manipulate or try to control your husband; only God controls.

5. Know you must always be independent to take care of you in case your husband won't.

6. Know your rights in your marriage by studying the word of the Lord and obeying it.

7. Know that you must develop love, confidence, courage, integrity, and respect to demand them.

8. Know that you too must have a minimum of a diploma and life degree.

9. Know that you must stay healthy and never give or take abuse of any kind.

10. Know who your real savior is, which is not your husband; nor are you his. *Jesus* is.

1. One of woman's big mistakes is expecting love before learning the respect of love. Also we expect a man to love us when we don't even know how to love ourselves or what love really is. Love is not just feeling romance and intimacy. From my experience it's mostly about sacrificing to do for others, especially when you don't feel like it, over and over again. Love is learning it's not about you all the time and that there is no *I* or *my* in a relationship, whether with a spouse, a friend, or whoever. It takes the two of you or all of you to make a marriage, friendship, or whatever relation good and healthy. But know how to always love God and keep Him first in your relationship and life, above everybody, including yourself and everything.

Warning, ladies: a man demands a woman, not a girl!

2. Ladies, get to know your husband well. Take the time, and give him time enough to get to know you too—that is, after you both have gotten to know God and His will for your relationship or marriage with each other. Know who you are and whose you are, bought and paid for in full, by the blood of *Jesus*, in order to discover how to develop your purpose here on earth. Learn who your enemies are and who the devil is so that you don't fall down when you should be standing up.

3. Okay, ladies, here is where we get ourselves in one of the biggest deceptions that the enemy (the devil) can use against us, and that is false images that appear in our minds. The trap is allowing them to have a field day. I can't begin to tell you how many times I have been wrong about the things that I thought negative about my husband without any proof, only to find out I was far off and wrong. I am sure you ladies can relate. We have

to realize the enemy doesn't want us together anyway because together we stand, divided we fall.

I had to come to reality about that and be honest with myself. So I took that tool away from the devil. I even got myself out of my own way because sometimes I would be blaming the devil, and it was me doing the damage in my own mind. Remember they say, "Believe half of what you see and none of what you hear, and think about everything you say, but don't say everything you think." We ladies take things way out of proportion, overanalyzing.

So give the gentleman a break when he deserves it. Stop saying hurtful things that you can't take back and doing things that end up costing you to lose a good thing. Learn when to fast from talking and just listen—you learn more that way—and respect your man before it escalates into an argument. We must be careful, learn our boundaries, and give them credit when it's deserved.

4. Ladies, when will we learn that we can't manipulate and control our man all the time? It's their job, with God's help, to control themselves, not ours. Besides, for those of you who always think you can, tell me: how is that working out for you? For many, many years I tried it, and it has never worked long for me. Oh, sure, it might work in the beginning of a relationship or marriage until they get you. But where does the love go after that? Well now, let's think back to the beginning and all the things we did to get him. That was easy because what we wanted in the beginning has no comparison to what we need after we get married. There is a lot more required from both after you get married.

5. What I am about to share with you here is good sound advice, *that goes for both the man and the woman. Demand that the both*

of you come to the table before a relationship/marriage even begins to discuss that you expect these things from each other:

A. *Love for Jesus and spiritual grounding*

B. *Love for yourself and then each other*

C. *A job*

D. *A house and furniture*

E. *A car*

F. *Good health*

G. *Auto, health, and life insurance*

H. *Savings*

I. *Budget in order*

J. *And last but not least, goooood credit*

I didn't. Don't make the same mistake I did. And even though my husband and I have it together now and are doing pretty well in all those categories, it was very hard and took a very long time. *I give you this sound advice so that in case, God forbid, something happens to one of you, the other will be able to carry on with no problems. Whether one passes away, gets a serious illness, or just for whatever reason leaves the relationship or marriage, that in itself is going to be hard enough to deal with. You won't have to get ready if you stay ready.*

I wish someone had taught me that before I entered into a relationship, let alone my marriage. I have friends who feel trapped still today because they didn't have this sound advice before their relationships or marriages.

6. Please, please know how to become a spouse by research on each other before starting a relationship or marriage. *Hold each other accountable* to read, study, and obey God's word, and let His will be done in your healthy relationship or marriage. The instructions are all in the Bible.

I've heard people say there is no manual on how to be married and raise children. I beg to differ; yes, there is. The book of Ephesians, for example, addresses everyone's obligations in the family: husband, wife, and children. The book of Proverbs is bursting with such wisdom. Remember that only what you do for God will last. It is never too late to get your house, relationship, and marriage in order with God's help. Just know you have to keep it in order for the rest of your lives.

It is not good for man to be alone; nor is it for woman. It is lonely at the top by yourself, and for sure it's lonely at the bottom. Learn how to get along with the opposite sex for marriage the way God intended. It is hard but doable. Settling for the same sex seems easier because the same sex understands each other. But don't give up on learning how to get along with the opposite. When you learn how to work it out, it will all come naturally without doubts, thoughts of "woulda, coulda, shoulda," or guilty feelings. And you reap the benefits as intended, God's way.

7. Probably the most important thing to do for your self-esteem is for you each to develop a character who has wisdom, knowledge, honor, respect, intelligence, integrity, and love for yourselves and for God first. In order for your relationship or marriage to be completed, you need these things to be a part of your package—for you first, and *demand* it of the other.

8. Get as much practice as you can from your immediate family. Try very hard always to get along with everyone in your family because developing good relationships should start at home. Then follow up on getting along with your distant relatives, friends, boss, co-workers, and so forth. If you can't get along with any of these groups of people, you might think twice about getting married because it will be far more challenging to be in a marriage relationship.

9. Never settle for someone who doesn't know and love God more than himself or others because it won't be a pleasant relationship or marriage. Be careful of people who have experienced a mental, physical, emotional, or financial collapse or been in a sexual abuse relationship. Make sure you know what you're getting into before pursuing more with them because they are already fragile and don't need you coming into their lives to play with their heart, mind, body, and soul.

Remember—what goes around comes around. Never abuse or tolerate any abuse; it is totally unacceptable. Everyone deserves a second chance; if you do pursue them, come with plenty of unconditional love, patience and wisdom to understand them, especially if they already have children. *Demand they do the same for you* because if they disrespect family and friends, you're next.

Before committing to each other, make sure you are equally yoked to prevent separation or divorce. Check everything out, and I mean turn over every rock. If they have nothing to hide, they shouldn't mind, and neither should you. I wish someone had taught me these things before I got married. Had I known then what I know now, I would only have gotten married once, as it was intended. So, my sisters in Christ, and anyone who is reading this book, I'm here on this beautiful day of July 28, 2017, in Las Vegas, Nevada, writing to you to pass along my wisdom, knowledge, talent, understanding, and experience to you instead of taking them to the grave.

10. Not keeping this demandment could make or break a relationship or marriage. You have to know your purpose for wanting to be in a relationship or marriage. Make sure it is because you and your partner are truly in love and want to get married, not because it is convenient or meets a need for a baby's daddy or mama or for money or any other materialistic, selfish reason. Make sure it is with someone God sends to you; do not pick him or her yourself.

One last thing I want to stress right now: never seek out in a person what only God can and would give you, and that is *salvation through His only begotten Son*. Your husband is not your savior, never has been, and never will be, and neither are you his. Only Jesus Christ can be!

THE 10 DEMANDMENTS
that children demand of their parents

1. Give love, honor, respect, understanding, and explanation to your children.
2. Give God the power to give you the wisdom to understand how to raise your children.
3. Give a fair punishment for discipline purposes when your children misbehave.
4. Give equal quality time to each child, as much as possible, for them to develop fully.
5. Give your children protection at all times, to shield them from hurt, harm, and danger.
6. Give your children the proper materials and tools to teach them how to be independent.
7. Give your children all the knowledge they need about the law to prevent imprisonment.
8. Give them the word of God so they and their families can learn their purpose in life.
9. Give them chores around the house to teach them responsibility and accountability.
10. Give them the love that God shows and tells you how to give from the Bible.

1. Countless children are hurting due to the lack of love, honor, respect, and validation from their moms and, especially, dads. It is crucial that both parents take full responsibility as their equal obligation to raise all their children, whether it be together or co-parenting. Both parents must be held accountable to raise the children until they are grown and independent, able to take care of themselves. Make sure the children also do their part to learn how to grow up and be accountable and independent because too many children don't ever want to grow up and leave their parents' home. They want and expect their parents to take care of them forever.

So we parents have to be role models and examples to our children at all times, so that they can grow up and learn their purpose. Once we have children, it is our immediate mission to take care of them appropriately. The children mimic almost everything they see and hear us do, so please watch what you do in front of your children. We want to make sure we teach them to raise each generation better than the ones before. Teach them according to the basic instructions in the Bible. Take them to a good, faith-based, believing church. There are many methods to learn about God nowadays with modern technology and social media. And parents, please take the time to teach them. Let there be no excuses.

2. Parents, please stop relying on schools, churches, recreation centers, community organizations, streets, jails, reformatories, and prisons to raise your children without your help. You are the key factor for them to get basic training, to learn wisdom, and to develop manners, discipline, respect, honor, and love for themselves and others in order to develop great character. You really shouldn't rely on outsiders to raise your children when it is your responsibility and obligation. They can fail you.

I know that it takes a village to raise a child, but come on, parents, do your job. It is not fair to put your responsibilities on someone else or the public. Make sure your children grow up to be good, productive members of society. And let all those other resources be a bonus to help your child grow up by doing their part; still, hold your child accountable, not the schools or all those others. It must come from home, starting with you, so they won't stray so far that they can't find their way back. Parents, pray to God to give you the wisdom to teach them how to understand their value in life. Pray He will help you be great examples to them by making sure you, as individuals and parents, have your own lives together and in order.

3. We parents must learn that our children are watching our every move when it comes to how we are treating our siblings. We have to be careful when disciplining children, so that each child is getting the appropriate punishment for their misbehavior, rather than one getting a harsher punishment than another. We must be fair when it comes to that. We also must be careful that the punishment doesn't turn into abuse to the child. Be a spiritual adult about the proper way to raise your children. Make sure they grow up to do the same for the generations to come.

Last but not least, make sure you two parents are on the same page when it comes to setting boundaries, and stand your ground in raising and disciplining the children. Don't let them start to manipulate and play you against each other. You want to make sure they grow up spiritually healthy.

4. Now let's talk about giving children equal quality time. It is far too easy to cheat our children out of it. I wish I'd known when I was raising my children what I know now. But I didn't know

better then, and now that I do, I want to pass it on to you, the way I wish someone back then had passed it on to me.

It is so very important to give your children that time at the right time, even if it seems like you don't have the time. You somehow make it happen. Everyone has the same 24 hours in a day, and some seem to make it happen; so can you. If you seem not to have enough time, that means you are going to have to make some changes and sacrifices in your schedule and life. That's what we must do when we choose to have children because they didn't choose to be here. I didn't realize that or even understand it when I was raising my children. Some of it came naturally but not enough as I understand it should have. I could easily have sacrificed more sleep and gotten more things done for my children. I could have sacrificed more of my time and myself for sure, had I only known better and put my children above my selfish interests.

I didn't realize then, but I do now. Spend equal quality time with your children after checking homework. It doesn't always take money, which was one of my excuses back then. The children just want your attention; it's as simple as playing and being around them as much as you can. It is crucial that you parents do that nowadays. I promise you that is a key part of their development.

5. Protect your children at all times as much as you honestly can, especially from family, relatives, friends, and all the bullies. That is where most of the betrayal, abuse, and molestation begins to happen. Don't forget the schools, day cares, and churches too. You, not someone else, are your children's first protectors from evil, hurt, harm, and danger.

Pray that God will be with you when parenting, to the best of your ability when it comes to your children. Teach them good morals and standards so they know right from wrong and how to be aware of their surroundings at all times. Teach them that there are heavy consequences to pay when they do wrong; if they do wrong, see that they face up and are accountable. Let them know that not everyone is their friend; teach them to recognize their enemies, especially the devil. Don't wait until they are too old; teach them at a very young age, as early as the age of two.

Talk, sing, and read to them when they are babies so they can learn how to hear. Don't wait for the schools, streets, and jails to teach them about life; you be the one. Spare your children all the drama by not neglecting to be an appropriate parent, showing and telling them that you love them like no other except God. Make sure the children have good meals to nourish them and that they are sent off to school with good attitudes. Check their progress reports, and go to the school meetings. Let the teachers know you are involved in being a team playing for your children's goal achievements.

6. Give your child the proper materials and tools to grow up to be independent. Starting from the womb, Mom, make sure you take great care of your body, knowing that whatever you take in goes through the child you are carrying. Make sure to get all your checkups before the baby and that the baby gets his or hers after delivery, including shots and dental and eye appointments. Dads, take your daughters out on dinner, movie, and dancing dates to show them how a gentleman should treat them. Mom, have those woman-to-woman talks way before puberty, when the hormones get to going every which way. Fathers, talk to your sons way before a nocturnal emission begins and about all the diseases.

7. As the children approach high school, prepare them for graduation. Don't wait until their senior year to make sure they have all the credits and the GPA that they need. Start at ninth grade to make sure they are taking their core courses way before twelfth grade. Teach them that school is a priority always before other extra activities and that a high school diploma is a necessity. If college is a choice, fine, but if they choose to start a career right out of high school, be there to help them as much as you can. I didn't attend college right away but started a thirty-year career right out of high school, so that could also be an option.

You parents also need to start teaching your children about the law at an early age, well before they get to young adulthood, so that they don't get tied up in the system. Teach them about the parties, alcohol, drugs, narcotics, marijuana, etc. Teach them how to respect driving before expecting to drive and the laws that apply to driving, both to prevent police brutality and so they can be independent. Spend a lot of one on young adult time with them. Make sure that they are comfortable enough to talk to you about any- and everything. Answer all their questions thoroughly and honestly even after they are gown up because you don't want them getting any grown-up bad advice in the streets or from their friends, who don't know any more than your children.

8. Teach them the word of the Lord by attending church and Bible study with them. Exercise what you learn in church, and be an example in showing them how to do the same. When you do, you and they can learn what your real purpose is for existing on this earth. That will keep them from being confused as to what life is all about so they can get started on their lifelong journey and not be a menace in society.

9. Give the children chores in and around the house, from an early age all the way up until they leave to start living on their own. Before they leave the house, also teach them how to respect money before expecting money and how to live off of it. Teach them to manage money as well as what tithing is all about and how it is better to give than to receive.

10. The bottom line is this: let's be responsible and accountable parents so our children can have a fair, healthy life mentally, physically, financially, and especially spiritually for them and the generations to come. Give them the love that God shows and tells you in the Bible how to give, from the two commandments in Mark 12:28–31. Teach them about salvation so that they can be saved and pass down to future generations how to be saved too (see Romans 10:9).

THE 10 DEMANDMENTS

*that parents demand
of their children*

1. Don't forget to love God above all and your neighbor as yourself.
2. Don't lie, steal, manipulate, or keep secrets from your parents.
3. Don't gossip about your parents to anyone.
4. Don't run away from your parents unless you're being abused or feel your life is threatened.
5. Don't ignore or get an attitude when you are being corrected or disciplined.
6. Don't betray your parents or lose their trust and bite the hand that feeds you.
7. Don't fear your parents; only fear God.
8. Don't disrespect your parents with rude body, eye, and tongue language.
9. Don't ever play your parents against each other.
10. Don't ignore that your days will be shortened if you disobey your parents.

1. Children, always keep the Lord our God above everybody and everything. Learn to love God with all your heart, soul, body, and mind. Love your neighbor as much as you love yourself if you want to keep strife out of your life and be blessed. Read all the Bible, and pay close attention to Matthew 22:36–40. Learn about these two commandments Jesus left as instructions for all of us who believe. God sent His only begotten Son to die so that we could live eternally.

2. Do not lie, deceive, or manipulate in order to get your way. Try not to have any secrets, period. Telling the truth is always best, even if you have to pay the consequences. Remember that the truth will always set you free and guiltless. Lies rob and steal and can kill. Lying really only cheats and especially cheats you if you're the one lying. Learn to be honest with yourself at all times. It can be a challenge, but you can do it. Once you learn how to conquer being honest with yourself at all times, you have won half the battle in any situation. It will become much easier to tell the truth to others as well.

3. Don't talk about your parents behind their backs to each other or to anyone else. Always speak to your parents in a very respectful, humble way about any issue that you have about them. After all, they are the ones who can resolve the issue better and faster than anyone you could ever tell. I'm sure they would rather you come to them instead of anyone else. Don't be so afraid of your parents that you can't speak to them about the hard stuff. There should not be anything that you can't talk to them about, no matter how big or small, even if it seems to be very uncomfortable.

4. Never run away from your fears or from home when things seem to get unbearable—unless you are truly being abused or your life is threatened. A lot of children seem to think things are better somewhere else and with someone else because they get older and don't feel like following the rules of the house that their parents have laid down anymore.

Notice with most children it starts in their teenage years. They get all the way to their teens and don't want to be told what to do anymore. Well, that is just a trap and disaster waiting to happen because the enemy, the devil, starts messing with your mind, telling and giving you false images in your head right around that age. You're coming into puberty, and your body starts to develop and change into a young adult. Your hormones take off and cause many changes in your body, especially in a female, and it's much different from the way it affects a male.

This is why it is so important to have a good enough relationship with your parents to talk to them about anything. It is your parents' responsibility to know when to start having certain talks about certain things. It's not the job of people in the streets, schools, media, TV, and social media just to name a few, to tell and show you the wrong things at the wrong time. Nine out of ten times your parents are only trying to do what's best for you.

5. Don't ignore or get an attitude when you are being corrected, disciplined, or educated by your parents. It is better to let them teach you out of love than someone who doesn't even know you, let alone love you. No one is going to love you like your parents do or should. Granted, not all parents are the best of parents, but most of them are trying to do the best that they know how. Make sure you're not the problem, and do your part.

6. Children, please don't betray your parents or lose their trust and bite the hand that feeds you. What a disappointment it is to parents who know they are bending over backward to make sure they are supporting their children the best way possible at the time, just to have them grow up and be unappreciative. The parents can never do enough to satisfy their children because of what the society, social media, or whoever and whatever has taken over their minds into thinking they should have more.

Instead of you children having a mind of your own, you tend to want what you think you should have just because your friends have whatever it is that they have. Learn to be thankful for what you've got. Some children in other countries don't have anything and are filthy poor compared to what you have. Remember—the hand that is feeding you is doing so out of love.

7. Do not fear your parents more than you fear God. In fact, fear only God! This is a different kind of fear than I mentioned in point 4. There may come a time when a circumstance happens and you are more fearful of your parents than you are of God.

For example: you do something that is out of your control, like have a car accident in your parents' automobile, and you lie about it, thinking they will never find out. And you lie about the accident not being your fault because you are so afraid of what your parents will do to you if they find out it was your fault, and they do find out. Instead of just telling the truth and trusting God, who said, "The truth will set you free."

Let's say it really was an accident, and it was your fault because you couldn't keep from hitting the car because you were trying to keep from hitting a bicyclist who swerved in front of you. That is something your parents would understand because the car you hit was only a fender bender. They would rather you hit the car instead of a human being. Therefore you didn't have to lie, and you could have trusted God and told the truth and not feared your parents so much, and it all would have been resolved. But instead you lied, feared your parents more than God, and got in trouble for lying—and now you can't drive the car anymore. You should have feared God and told the truth because God always brings the dark to the light. This is just a minor example; many times circumstances are much worse.

8. Watch your rude body language through your eyes, tongue, and head rolling or talking back under your breath just having to get the last word. That is disrespectful. I don't mind if you really have a point you want to make, but do it with respect. I realize sometimes children are wrongfully accused and deserve to defend themselves in a mannerly way because it could be that the parent is wrong. That is rare but possible. Just don't try to play your parents and insult their intelligence. And for sure, remember to never get physical or violent with your parents, again unless you have to protect yourself from a life-threatening or abusive situation. Learn how to communicate with your parents and establish a good relationship with them. Learn how to establish a good, healthy relationship with your friends and soul mate before getting married.

9. Don't ever play your parents against each other to try to get them to separate or divorce, especially if you are a stepchild to a stepparent. Learn your role in the relationship, and stay in your lane. Pray that God's will may be done in each other for a healthy family relationship.

10. Remember this, children, if you don't remember anything else. A child who disobeys their parents, days will be shorten. Read all about it in Exodus 20:12. God gave you children parents for a reason. When the parents raise their children the best they can and know how to, then the children should always want to obey the things they are told to do because parents know best. Also read the whole Bible, especially the book of Ephesians. You will learn by reading these references about how to get along with your parents and family. You will read about all family members and how they should conduct themselves in a family.

Children, be blessed!

THE 10 DEMANDMENTS
that I demand of myself

1. I demand of myself to put God first before everything and everybody forever.

2. I demand to love God number one, myself, spouse, children, relatives, and others in that order.

3. I demand to be honest with God number one, with myself, and with others in that order.

4. I demand to give and ask for forgiveness when necessary.

5. I demand to keep my body spiritually clean inside and the outside physically.

6. I demand to establish a relationship with God to get *my basic instructions*.

7. I demand to follow my Holy Spirit for guidance, left down here for me from *Jesus*.

8. I demand to live debt-free of all credit cards by 2018, realizing they are a bondage.

9. I demand to live the rest of my life as a servant to God with dignity and integrity.

10. I demand to surrender my life to God and follow my instructions from Him, to give everything that I have so that my spouse, my children, and generations to come, as well as you who are reading this book, can reap the benefits. Whatever wisdom, knowledge, talent, and experience I have, I understand that I am to pass it on to you, knowing I can't take it to the grave with me. I want to hear the words from God, *"Good and faithful servant!"*

1. I demand of myself to put God before anything and everybody at all times. I tried it the other way around, and it didn't work for me— just like it won't work for you. God made it perfectly clear that He is a jealous God. I got the message loud and clear and want to spare you as much as I can by making it clear to you. I can maybe help you a little if you allow me to. So I am asking you to read Exodus 34:14 (KJV).

God has blessed me so much since I learned to study His word to learn His will and His way for me, not my own. God loves me so much that He gave up His only begotten Son to die for me so I can have eternal life because He has risen and still today and forever, lives. Jesus, the Son of God, suffered and sacrificed everything for those who believe He is the Son of God.

I used to put people and things before God, but now I know better, so I do better. You too must learn this, and the sooner you do, the better your life will be too. My life now is peaceful and full of joy instead of drama. I'm happy and living abundantly because I discovered only God can make me happy; no other person or thing can.

I made a mistake for many years, trying to control my husband into making me happy, and it never worked. All along I didn't realize there was no way he could. I have my priorities straight now and sleep really well at night, to wake up to a blessed day, every day, giving all the glory and honor to God and my Lord and Savior, Jesus Christ— not to a human being who can and will fail me. I have a wonderful husband and beautiful family of generations to prove it. I belong to Remnant Ministries under the beautiful pastors Mrs. Felicity and Mr. Randall Cunningham, who are great teachers of God's word.

2. I demand of myself to love God, myself, my husband, family, friends, and others in that order. I will never leave God because now I surely know better. Loving God and choosing Him because He first chose me is one of the most valuable lessons I have ever learned. I am here today paying it forward to you by telling you that you should do the same, just as I have told my husband, six children, twenty-eight grandchildren and thirteen great-grandchildren.

3. I demand to stop cheating myself by staying true to God and myself and then others. I refuse to live a life of lies and secrets that rob, steal, and kill. I enjoy now living a life of truth that sets me free because I believe in the one who brought the *truth, Jesus Christ!*

4. I demand of myself to forgive so I can keep my freedom by being forgiven. I'm glad I learned how to say, "I am sorry; please forgive me." I can think of only one person on this whole earth who is allowing the enemy to go through her to get to me, but it will never break my vow to God first and her second to always love her. I just refuse to allow the enemy (the devil) to overpower me though because "I can do all things through Christ which strengtheneth me" (Philippians 4:13 KJV)—another valuable lesson that I have learned.

I am even on speaking terms with my exes, by whom I have children because I want to be an example to my children that we can all still get along in spite of our differences. I taught my children, just as I have learned, how to be independent because there may be many times and people that you won't get along or agree with. So have your own mind, house, job, car, and relationship with God and the Holy Spirit, who will guide you through, all the way out of here. *Amen!* That defeats a lot of arguing, fighting, and killing each other. Don't let the sun go down when you're angry on the inside.

5. I demand to keep my life as pure and clean as possible, mind, body, and soul. I don't allow false images to orchestrate my brain. I don't allow sin to reside in my soul, and I definitely watch my intake with beverages and food to avoid as many toxins as I exert my willpower to refuse. And I certainly don't do any kind of alcohol or drugs; nor do I smoke. I tried a few of those things, and my body said no. I listen to my body through the Holy Spirit, aka my alarm, intuition, and protector after the first time, when it warned me about those things, or any kind of hurt, harm, and danger. You should try it also; I highly recommend it.

I know for a fact, that is why today, at sixty-six years old, with all the family I've mentioned and a thirty year career, I am in great shape. All my vital numbers are where they should be. I only take one medication which the doctors say I have to take for the rest of my life, due to a bad choice I once made in my life. And that was before I accepted the wisdom of God. First time, shame on me; second time, shame of it. I get it now: "Thank you, Jesus."

I practice to take very good care of my life so my family doesn't have to. I wouldn't want to put that burden on any of them and have asked them to please not put it on me. No stress, no mess. Let us all just take good care of our temples, which belong to God in the first place. But recognize that the enemy uses false images as one of his biggest tools to destroy us; do not underestimate his tactics. Then there are the ones we create ourselves and blame the devil or our enemies. Remember to fill your body up with the Holy Spirit to keep and guide you all the way.

6. I demand that closer walk with God on a daily and hourly basis, even minute-by-minute and down to the second in our relationship, for my better understanding of what my purpose is for being here on earth. Now that I understand how to receive it from God, I live every day as if it is my last day. With no doubt that I will meet my Creator and Savior, I don't fear death, life, people, or things. I only fear my God. Yes, I am a God-fearing woman. If you want to know why, I'd rather tell you in person. If you want to know, e-mail me at loretta7@cox.net; I'd love to share my reasons with you.

Of course because I am human I may get frightened of something, making me afraid or anxious, but that's not fear; there is a difference. Please recall the little example of that in the demandments that I wrote for the children. I feel that at sixty-six I am at the prime time of my life, which God has blessed me by prolonging so that I may do some of the things that I want to do because I was obedient in raising my six gifts of lives that He trusted me with. I feel like I am only thirty and have a good thirty more years at least. My mother lived into her eighties and my father into his nineties, and they didn't even get to establish a relationship with God the way I learned how; either no one taught them how, or they just wouldn't accept it.

I am looking forward to those years to make the best yet to come. G'N' I (God and I) is my logo for those of you who don't already know me and haven't read my first book, called *Give Me My Flowers While I Live and I'll Do the Same for You*. Whenever you know of me to use the word *I*, *my*, or *me*, that's who I am referring to. Please remember that. So all those instances of *I*, *my*, and *me* that you already read through so far and didn't know, now you know.

7. I demand of myself to let God lead the rest of my life, for the duration of my journey here on earth, and to use me so that He can be seen through me serving His people in action.

8. I demand peace in my life and in all my surroundings. I love to help people who want to be helped because someone helped me get to where I am. I've learned that it is impossible to help those who do not want to help themselves.

I realize God will be very proud if you can help the ones that are very difficult to help because they just don't know any better. However, they still have to want the help. You can't force the ones who refuse to surrender their life over to God—God chose them, but they won't choose God in return. I know that seems a little hard to understand. I have tried helping people by force, and it doesn't work that way. I learned the hard way; you don't have to. Just understand the difference between your job and God's job. God doesn't need your help. He does put us in people's path to help them and people in our path to help us. But the help must be received. If you try to help someone, and it gets all difficult and confusing, that might be you in God's way because God is not a God of confusion.

Let me explain how I got in my own way of blocking the peace and blessings out of my life. I allowed the enemies (the devil) to visit me. But I learned how to get rid of them because I no longer felt at peace. Debt is one of my enemies. I see now why God doesn't want us to be in debt. Here I am trying to serve God's people He sent into my path, and debt caused a huge distraction. It didn't stop me from serving my purpose, but it slowed me down. I have a good handle on it now, but I demand to get rid of it, and I will by 2018. It is the only distraction left in my life. G'N'I have already eliminated the rest, and that is why I am writing this book, to forward God's wisdom and pass to you the know-how to live life abundantly. I will have a whole lot more time in 2018 to help those who want to receive the help. I am and have been living the abundance for a while now.

9. I demand to keep loving God and keep Him first in my life to stay on the right track. It is easy to trip and stumble and even fall; just get back up again, and lean forward so you don't fall back into your old bad habits, addictions, relationships, and debt—just to name a few.

10. I demand to keep following the two *commandments* that *Jesus* left for me, so that all the works in action that flow out of my following them can trickle down to my family, the generations to come, and you, long after I am gone to glory. I feel like G'N'I have already achieved everything that I could even imagine but want to use every bit of what I have left for God to use me up. I know God and have introduced my family and you to Him. I of course have accepted Him, and I hope they and you do too.

God bless you all, and thank you for your support!

THE 10
Do Not Settle for Less List

1. Do not settle for less than you are worth, but know your value.

2. Do not settle for excuses, copouts, and a bunch of *I can'ts*.

3. Do not settle for someone who won't apologize or forgive.

4. Do not settle for someone who won't nourish you back to health.

5. Do not settle for someone who won't sacrifice for you.

6. Do not settle for someone who fears everything but God and doesn't love God.

7. Do not settle for someone who is afraid or just won't commit to marriage.

8. Do not settle for people who don't love themselves, let alone love you.

9. Do not settle for someone who abuses you in any form or fashion—*intolerable*.

10. Do not settle for someone who will not submit to God but asks you to submit to him.

1. Do not settle for less than you know that you are worth; know your value. This applies to everyone. If you are saved and a child of God, you are a King or Queen of God's. If you carry yourself as such, people will treat you as such. People only do to you what you allow them. If you produce good fruit, you will receive good fruit. Demand to be treated like a child of God as you treat others as a child of God.

Raise a generation of good fruit and demand each generation after yours do the same. This is a way to break generations and generations of those cursed by alcoholism, drug addiction, smoking, obesity, etc. Our families don't have to continue the generational pattern and repeat the cycle of bad diets, toxic intakers, and failed marriages. We can be the one to start the new generation in our families to break the old-time religions and start a new relationship with our God, one at a time.

We are created to have the best but often settle for less. So many fathers and mothers fail their children because their parents failed them. Stop the madness, and learn how to be a great parent. There are no more excuses when we have abundant teachings and examples; we *can* learn to be great parents. People like myself and many others are putting out material such as this book you are reading to give you direction on how we all can do better in raising generations of our people God intended for us to be.

Mothers, stay there to teach your daughters what only a mother can. Fathers, commit to hang in there and teach your sons what only a father can. And then let us come together and be the family that we were created to be. Put some God back in our homes, churches, governments, and schools, as well as our finances, our health, and our lives. Notice the fact that it just doesn't work when we don't have the Creator of all things in our calculation; things just don't and won't ever add up, because we can do nothing without God. Remember— only what you do for God will last. Read the, KJV Bible; it's all in there.

2. Let us stop copping out, running, and hiding from our responsibilities and be accountable to God and each other. Quit with all the excuses and all the *I can'ts*. It's not that you *can't*; most of the time, it's that you *won't* because you just simply don't want to. Stop lying to yourself and others. Start your generation of being men and women who *can and will* turn this out-of-control, mixed-up dysfunctional world upside down and inside out. There sure can't be a beginning of change in your generation if you don't start it.

So what are you waiting for? If you don't know how to get started, e-mail me. I have learned how to start breaking a lot of curses in my generation, starting with myself and my immediate family. It can be done; I am a witness. I began to stop many bad habits and start a lot of good ones. In my first book I show and tell of the curses that have been broken in our generation of families, starting with me. So kick Satan out of the way in the name of Jesus. Swallow your pride, surrender to God, and learn how to sacrifice. It's not about you all the time, especially when you have chosen to take on a family. And let's start raising some great, productive families in this society.

3. We all must learn how to say we're sorry and forgive one another. We must realize that the best way to get along is to allow one another to be who they are, which is who you are not. God made us all equal and different at the same time, for His own reasons. Respect that about each other. Don't try to force

someone to be who they are not. That goes for husbands and wives, as well as your children. Let us all be who God intended.

4. If you are in a relationship or marriage, love each other enough before you get into that relationship or marriage to discipline yourself, to make sacrifices. For example, if one of you gets a chronic illness, stay and help through the healing. Do not leave your partner who has become disabled for any reason. Be man and woman enough to stay, for better or worse, until death do you part. *Now that's love!*

5. Let me elaborate on sacrifice. The above also goes for your family, especially the children. Never leave a parent alone if one or more children become ill or disabled. It's definitely going to take the strength of the two of you along with God's blessings. There are going to be many, many times in any kind of relation and marriage when you will have to be willing to show your love by your willingness to sacrifice.

Make sure you know the meaning of sacrifice. In a nutshell, it means doing for others when you really are able to but simply don't feel like it or just don't want to. Don't be selfish and choose not to sacrifice. *Don't settle for anyone like that!* They are not worth anything in life if they won't learn how to sacrifice. And take it from our Lord and Savior Jesus Christ—*the greatest sacrificer that ever has and ever will be, or would and could.* That is who you should try to mimic; I do.

6. Don't settle for anyone who is not God-fearing enough to fear Him if you don't do His will. His will must be done in *all* things and ways in our life, or there could be heavy consequences. Of

course God gives us choice, one of the most valuable gifts He could give us. But we must choose wisely, and wisdom comes only from God. How will you know that if you never get to love, learn, and study God? The answer is, you won't. That is why it is *crucial* that you learn about your Creator. Don't block your blessing by putting off learning where and how your blessings flow.

7. Definitely don't settle for someone who is afraid to commit to marriage but wants to just shack up and live together. Either they come all the way in, or they get out of the way of someone who is willing and not afraid to make a complete commitment. It's that simple. The way to make sure you're going to do your best is to make that commitment. Otherwise, don't kid yourself. If they don't commit, it is a sure sign that they have doubts already about the relationship or marriage, giving it a slim chance of surviving.

You need someone who is going to give their fair share when you are committing to do so. The key is, before you commit, to make sure you both are believers of God so that your relationship or marriage is not unequally yoked. Being equally yoked is the *demand* you want for your protection in your relationship or marriage. You can't be afraid you'll fail by thinking you will. As where the mind goes in thinking the body will follow. Think positive, think God, trust God, and let God direct your *relationship or marriage.* Follow Him through the Holy Spirit left here by His only begotten Son, *Jesus Christ, and let Him guide you all the way. Amen!*

8. Do not settle for someone who doesn't learn how to love God or themselves let alone you. So how can they learn? As they say by the B.I.B.L.E.—Basic Instructions Before Leaving

Earth. Please let this be a *warning!* A person can't give what they don't have.

9. *Do not settle for abuse in any way, shape, form, or fashion, nada, zip, zero, not ever at all! I cannot put enough emphasis on this. Do not settle for less.*

10. Do not ever settle for someone who would ask you to submit to them before they submit to God first.

THE 10 MOST CHALLENGING

relationship or marriage tests that you will likely face

1. Faith
2. Emotions
3. Family
4. Friends
5. Health
6. Responsibilities
7. Deception
8. Debt
9. Patience
10. Death

1. Your biggest challenge in your relationship or marriage is going to be a lack of patience. I guarantee all of these ten topics will be experienced during your relationship or marriage. So before you think or say, *if I could have, I would have, or I should have, let me tell you that I would, will, can, and did!*

Let me explain. I developed enough faith to believe that I can learn how to keep my relationship or marriage this time. I say "this time" because I've been married three times. I almost thought it was impossible to stay in my marriage after the third time and almost gave up on trying a fourth. I had already determined not to give up on marriage because I don't want to grow old by myself. Besides, God assured me I could have a successful marriage and live life abundantly. I was searching for that.

I had already achieved just about everything else in life that I wanted, but learning *how to get along with the opposite sex* became one of my biggest challenges in life (even bigger than birthing a child, and I know about that because I birthed five sons and one daughter). When I tell you it took all the faith that I could mustard seed up to believe that I could, I *did* learn how to get along with my husband, the opposite sex.

What I am about to tell you is for both women and men. I understand that it seems logical that a man understands a man better than he does a woman because a woman understands a woman better than a man would. So it makes sense that it would be much easier to get along with the same sex. However, that was not God's intention, which is why I was determined to do it God's way. I knew I couldn't go wrong if I just figured it out, and I did.

Keep the faith, and never give up. Never give up on the opposite sex. God never intended for us to turn to the same sex for a soul-mating marriage. No pain, no gain. I will admit there was a lot of pain. But I made it.

2. Emotions can't get in the way as we women especially allow them to. We have to stop operating on feelings and learn how to depend on our intuition—you know, the Holy Spirit. It will guide, warn, protect, and direct you to make the right decision every time. Again, this is hard to do but can be done. Try it, and you'll see. Then compare the difference between following emotions and following the Holy Spirit.

I know because I have experienced a couple of times acting out my emotions and made myself look like a fool and lost the game of life. When I tried trusting and leaning on my Holy Spirit, I won the game. I felt good about winning, after getting over the momentary uncomfortable feeling of not trusting the outcome. You ladies and gentlemen know what I am speaking of. You know those games in our relationship or marriage that we tend to play on each other because our relationship or marriage is still so fresh and new. So we try each other out by playing games to see what we can and cannot get away with. Those kinds of games can make or break up a relationship or marriage.

3. Oh, how family loves to get in the middle of our relationships and marriages, especially our in-laws. Let's admit there are advantages and mostly disadvantages. If we as a couple did our due diligence in our relationship and marriage in the first place, we wouldn't even need to involve them in our business, except for inviting them to the wedding to play their parts. If we took the time to really get to know each other and each made sure the other did their research—maybe even became friends first instead of lovers—the marriage would have a solid foundation.

4. Friends most of the time mean well but give bad advice. Make sure you have established a good relationship even with your friends. Many who you think are friends just might be counterfeits or even enemies. They tend to influence our decision making when they should just pray for us, especially when they've never been in a relationship or marriage themselves. So let's talk about friends getting in the way or their reasons for wanting to be involved so much in our relationships or marriages.

Real friends may be sincere, but the so-called friends may be on a mission to break you up rather than supporting your togetherness. One reason could be that they are jealous because they are not in a relationship. Or they could be more interested in your mate than you think. Maybe, just maybe they are jealous of the time you take from them to spend with your mate. Whatever the reason for them to be a part of your decision-making when it comes to your mate, just be careful and make sure they are genuine. Never tell too much about your mate, which can influence spark your friend's more than legit interest in your mate (even though it is never legit). Never take their advice when it comes to separating or divorcing. Always try to get some genuinely spiritual marriage advice before getting married. And if you're just in a relationship, get some marriage counseling before you get married.

5. Health is one of the most important things in a relationship or marriage. Neither of you should even enter into one unless you are in the best of health. As a matter of fact, that should be an individual priority before you even consider mating up with someone else. When you're in a bad health situation, it is not ever fair to yourself (let alone the other person) for you to involve someone else. Handle your business, and get well. *Demand a physical report from each other before getting emotionally, physically, mentally, and especially sexually involved with another individual.*

6. Responsibility and accountability seems to be one of a man's hardest challenges. I wish someone, anyone, could explain that one to me. If you're reading this book and you know, please e-mail me and solve that mystery for me. I have a lot of personal thoughts about it, but I am not a man. I need a man to show and tell me why it is that you have such a hard time committing to being responsible and accountable, especially with women and children, when you're in a relationship/marriage. I am serious about this. I surely don't want to start a bashing conversation about this, as a matter of fact, gentlemen, I am on your side. I would love for any man who is up to the challenge to come and co-write a book about this with me. Please contact me at your earliest convenience.

In the meantime I would like to let you men know: if you are just intimidated by all the responsibility, so are we women. But once we bear children, we don't have much choice other than to be accountable and committed to you and especially the children. I mean, it is a huge responsibility for the both of us and can even get overwhelming, but when we get tired and weary, *Jesus* carries us when we don't even know He is doing it (in case you ever wondered just how we women do it). We are never left alone.

And one other thing: I know how some mothers are just too difficult to deal with, so it seems best to walk away, leaving mother and children behind. But that is never best. Where there is a will, there is a way, and that way is *God's will. Seek Him first!*

7. Deception is a scary word. It even sounds wicked. It seems to happen to women more often than to men, I've heard, because there are seven to ten more women to one man. I've heard that women are getting so desperate that they are even willing to share men. I've even heard that women don't want a

committed relationship or marriage anymore; they just want to be romantically and sexually satisfied. No matter what the case may be, deception goes on at an alarming rate, with both men and women doing it.

But consider this: they say there are more men doing it than women, but every man who does it has a woman to do it with, so I don't necessary believe that. What I've never understood is why someone has to cheat, other than greed, when they are in a marriage. I do understand there may be children involved, and they try to stay for the children's sake. But it usually ends up getting pretty messy and causes more bad than good anyway.

If one seems to no longer be satisfied, instead of leaving, figure it out by *seeking wisdom from God first! Let God always be your out, and you will always stay in, especially if you have children. Stop copping out.* God is your ammunition to fight the enemy (the devil). When he tries to use deception to offer reasons for a separation or divorce, don't allow it.

8. Debt was one of my enemies for a long time until I, learned how to conquer it (really G'N'I). I can't blame this one on the devil, because I knew how debt can put you in bondage, and I ignored that fact more than once. I usually don't trip over the same obstacle twice. But finances seem to be a little more difficult for me to wrap my head around, partly because the banking and lending institutions keep changing the rules and regulation for the minorities. Every time I learn my way through one thing, they change or raise the scale or the debt ratio, require a higher FICA score, or do something else. I had to figure it out because most of all God doesn't want me to be in bondage with all the missions that he has prepared for me to accomplish. And debt

can be a huge distraction. But I have it under control and will be debt free very soon.

So you heard it from me: if you're not in debt don't get in debt. Bad debt can affect your FICA score, and that can raise costs on auto insurance, interest rates, and a lot more. I don't want that. Debt is also one of the reasons for divorce and illnesses. I used to let money manage me; now I manage money. I learned that through tithing. I experienced the difference between tithing and not. I learned that I can trust God's money that He gave me to manage along with God. Try tithing for six months and then not tithing for six months, and let me know how that works out for you. *Warning: debt causes stress, and stress causes mess! Get rid of it! It is one of my 10 Demandments.*

9. What is patience? What is love? Is it feelings, romance, emotions, mental, pleasure, or intimacy (just to name a few)? I've heard love is many things. But I've learned that love only means one thing to me that matters. And that is *God is love!* How about that? God's love beats out all the above because God's love is unconditional. God's love has more *patience* than anyone. He's all the love I need, want, depend on, trust, and live for. I don't need any other's validation. More than anything, I practice love and patience. It is part of what I see us human beings lacking.

10. Why do people fear the dead more than the living, when only the living can hurt us? And why do people have such a hard time dealing with death, if we believe in eternal life? Why are some people worth more dead than alive, if supposedly they were so loved by loved ones? Why do some people get more flowers when they are dead than when they were alive, if people really cared that much about them? Why do some dead people get more

respect when they are dead than when they were alive, if they were such productive citizens on earth? Why do some people get more visitors at their funeral than they got through all the years they were alive, if people cared so much? Why do some people prefer to be cremated than buried if it doesn't matter and you won't know anyway?

Last but not least, why do some people mourn for so long after someone dies if they really believe they are with our Creator and it should be a time to rejoice? Death can leave us stuck in a dark place for a long time if we love our loved ones too much, once they have passed away. One may ask, how much is too much? *I say if you loved them more than you love GOD, whether they be dead or alive, that's too much! Nothing and no one comes before God and should be loved before or more than God! (Examine yourself.)*

Life and death can be a challenge in our life if we don't really understand it. I don't know how it would feel to lose a child, because all mine are still living (thank God). But I have lost parents, siblings, and others, so I have experienced death. I once was ill and thought I was dying. That was when I searched for God more than ever, and I found Him.

I've never feared death. I think it is because my father used to take us to funerals a lot when we were children. When I was ill, I studied the Word and learned a lot about how God's concept works. I learned His will for *me* and that He has already written my life from the beginning to the end. It is up to me by choice whether I am going to follow His path that He has already written for me or get off the path. I choose to follow and stay on it as much as I humanly know how by following my Holy Spirit guidance. So far, so good. And yes, I stumble and fall sometimes, but I never stay down. I will always get back up again.

When studying about God, I learned that He is the beginning and the end, Alpha and Omega, and that all power is in His hands. He is the only one who has all power over life and death; therefore I do not fear death. I believe that all my generations and I belong to God, and whenever He chooses to take them from this earth, He is not taking them from me, because they were never mine in the first place. We all belong to God, bought and paid for by the blood of *Jesus Christ, our Lord and Savior!*

So fear not death. I will pass this down to my children and generations to come so that they too will respect death but not fear it. I have prepared my family for my death, and I am prepared for theirs. *I think when we get too far off track, God has a way of getting our attention. He either allows us to get locked up in jail due to a bad choice we've made or lays us down with illness because most likely we chose not to take very good care of His/our temples, or if we've done enough on earth and it is our time, He allows us to go home to Him to glory!—just to name a few.*

Peace, my brothers and sisters in Christ! May God bless us all!

HOW YOU KNOW
you have arrived in a successful relationship or marriage

You will feel and look great. You will wake up in the morning first thanking God that you are alive and well. You will thank Him for all five of your senses, your organs and limbs, and every breath that you take. If you're married, you can look over and touch and feel your spouse, if they are lying next to you. You will look all around your home and thank God for everything in it and that it is still standing in peace. You will thank God for no bad news through the night from a phone call. Then you will rise and thank Him for letting everything work on your body without any aches or pains whatsoever, not even a scratch or a hangnail. And then thank Him that your piping is working so you can use the bathroom.

You will just thank Him for your abundant life as promised and for all the peace around you bundled up in Him! Amen.

My husband and I have been through thick and thin, good and bad, illness and now health. We have worked many years, starting at the age of sixteen up into our fifties and have now retired. We came together with what we had to bring to the table and learned to work out everything and got married. We are now successfully married and living a very blessed abundant life, not needing a thing. We are a testimony that if you work, you shall eat, by our test. We are a witness that you can live life abundantly if you love the Lord and obey His word. And because we both learned how to submit to God first and then each other, we enjoy everyday life, as Joyce Meyer tells us to.

Before I close out this book, I have to share this one thing with you that might one day help your relationship or marriage.

While my husband and I are still together after seventeen years, you should know that no one stays together that long without a lesson learned to share with someone to help them through what might seem to be a hard relationship or marriage too. So here it is: When my husband and I got married, I first asked my pastor at the time to counsel us. I remember him telling me something that to this day I believe is one of the reasons my husband and I are still together.

He told us that there is always going to be one or two things about your spouse that is probably never going to change that you don't like about them. For sixteen years there was only one thing about my husband that almost broke up our marriage, but I hung on to those words my pastor said because I decided to marry anyway even though my pastor warned me that this thing I didn't like might never stop. To this day it still hasn't stopped, but it no longer is a threat to our marriage because it has gotten better.

Before I tell you what this thing is, I want to let you know that I literally have a really good husband, and any normal woman would love to have a husband like mine. I was normal before I married my husband; however, I am no longer normal. Let me explain why. Before I married my husband, I didn't know God the way I do now. I didn't know then what I know now. I didn't know what all I was entitled to then that I now know I am entitled to. As a normal woman that I was then, I didn't realize I am an heir of God's because I am a child of God, which entitles me to life abundantly.

So I say that to say this: that one thing that my husband wasn't giving me, I felt was the last thing I needed for my life abundant. I didn't feel happy in my marriage just because of this one thing, even though my husband has always given me everything else. That one thing was that I wanted my husband at home in my bed every night. I made it perfectly clear that that was one of the main reasons why I got married in the first place. In other words, you ladies and gentlemen know when you come to the table way before you get married and you tell each other what you want out of the marriage.

And you discuss what are deal breakers in a relationship long before you get married.

Are you with me so far? Now my husband cooks, cleans, shops, babysits my granddaughter, drives me around, washes the cars, fixes the things in the house … you name it, he does it. He does everything except that one pet peeve that I have, not coming home and being in my bed, okay our bed, at a decent hour of the night. That one thing hunted our marriage for sixteen years. I let the enemy/devil see me wear that anger about that one thing on my sleeve for sixteen years. I took it personally even though his mother told me not to take it personally because he had been doing that since he was sixteen, and that was why she put him out of her house. She said he'd always liked running the streets.

I tried to control and manipulate him for sixteen years about that. I prayed to God to take it away and then I would take it back from God. That went on for sixteen years. I finally decided after it almost broke us up to let it go once and for all and just settle for meeting him halfway. And although he still goes out, he does come home at a somewhat decent hour. Of course I still don't like that he goes out, but all his good outweighs that one bad. Pray for me, y'all, that one day he'll stop.

The good news is I have turned it over to God. And I don't get angry anymore about it. I held myself/G'N'I accountable to sticking to the marriage and not being another mad black woman going wide and being another statistic of a divorce. I didn't give the enemy (the devil) what he really wanted, which was a breakup, because together we stand, divided we fall. And besides, it would have been my loss. So G'N'I won the war after sixteen years of battle. I can still hear the words of my pastor in my ears today.

My purpose of telling you this is to let you know there may be just one thing dingalinging around in your marriage, and you're concentrating on having a good relationship or marriage. You might want to take this testimony into consideration and save your relationship or marriage too, especially if you know it is a good one. And besides, if I had just turned it over to God and left it with God sixteen years ago, this probably would have been over in sixteen seconds. I have now let go and let God, and I am going to wait until God works on God's time to stop him completely. And to be honest, that is nowhere near grounds for a divorce anyway. Even though I suspected cheating, I never found any proof.

My husband did end up getting into a little trouble that found him out there. He always used to say, "I'm not doing nothing wrong," when in reality I did find some inappropriate texts in his phone. I had to make a few calls and stripped his phone, and they and he stopped it. That is why I didn't want him out there in the wee hours in the first place. Trouble will find you.